THE
APOSTLESHIP

THE
APOSTLESHIP

by Bruce E. Dana

CFI
Springville, Utah

© 2006 Bruce Dana
All rights reserved.

No part of this book may be reproduced in any form whatsoever, whether by graphic, visual, electronic, film, microfilm, tape recording, or any other means, without prior written permission of the publisher, except in the case of brief passages embodied in critical reviews and articles.

ISBN 13: 978-1-55517-899-5
ISBN 10: 1-55517-899-5

Published by CFI, an imprint of Cedar Fort, Inc., 925 N. Main, Springville, UT, 84663
Distributed by Cedar Fort, Inc., www.cedarfort.com

LIBRARY OF CONGRESS CATALOGING-IN-PUBLICATION DATA

    Dana, Bruce E.
      The Apostleship / by Bruce E. Dana.
        p. cm.
      Includes bibliographical references.
      ISBN 1-55517-899-5
      1. Mormon Church--Apostles. 2. Church of Jesus Christ of Latter-day Saints--Government. I. Title.

    BX8657.D36 2006
    262'.149332--dc22

                                2006014948

Cover design by Nicole Williams
Cover design © 2006 by Lyle Mortimer
Printed in the United States of America

10 9 8 7 6 5 4 3 2 1

Printed on acid-free paper

TABLE OF CONTENTS

Preface	vii
Acknowledgments	xiii
Calling of the Jewish Twelve	1
The Nephite Twelve	15
How Joseph Smith Was an Apostle	23
The Quorum of the Twelve Apostles	37
The Twelve and the Kirtland Temple	45
The Faithful Six	53
The Twelve Lead the Church	63
The Twelve as the First Presidency	79
Apostles Not of the Twelve	91
The Twelve Speak about Their Calling	101
Meeting the Needs of the Growing Church	151
The Twelve Are Chosen to Be Special Witnesses	159
Notes	181
Index	197
About the Author	203

Preface

Questions Concerning the Apostleship

Faithful members of the Church wholeheartedly sustain the First Presidency and the Quorum of the Twelve Apostles as prophet, seers, and revelators. Though much has been revealed about their calling, many members of the Church have a limited knowledge about the apostleship.

It is therefore appropriate to ask the following questions of each member of the Church: What do you know about the Jewish Twelve? What do you know about the Nephite Twelve? How was Joseph Smith an Apostle? What does the title Apostle mean? How were the first members of the Twelve Apostles chosen in this dispensation? What does it mean to be a prophet, seer, and revelator? What transpired with the Twelve Apostles when Joseph Smith was martyred? How long did the Twelve Apostles function as the First Presidency of the Church? How are members of the Twelve Apostles called in our day? What is the duty and responsibility of an Apostle? What transpires with the Twelve Apostles when a president of the Church dies in our day?

The Title "Apostle"

Concerning the title "Apostle," we read these informative words written by Elder Bruce R. McConkie:

> This is the supreme office in the church in all dispensations because those so ordained hold both the fulness of

the priesthood and all of the keys of the kingdom of God on earth. The President of the Church serves in that high and exalted position because he is the senior Apostle of God on earth and thus can direct the manner in which all other Apostles and priesthood holders use their priesthood. An Apostle is an ordained office in the Melchizedek Priesthood, and those so ordained . . . are set apart as members of the Quorum of the Twelve and are given keys and power to preside over the church and kingdom and regulate all of the affairs of God on earth.

Apostles are "special witnesses of the name of Christ in all the world." They are also "a Traveling Presiding High Council, to officiate in the name of the Lord, under the direction of the Presidency of the Church, agreeable to the institution of heaven; to build up the church, and regulate all the affairs of the same in all nations, first unto the Gentiles and secondly unto the Jews." (D&C 107:23, 33)[1]

In a statement that was approved by the First Presidency, Elder James E. Talmage wrote:

The title "Apostle" is one of special significance and sanctity; it has been given of God, and belongs only to those who have been called and ordained as "special witnesses of the name of Christ in all the world, thus differing from other officers in the Church in the duties of their calling." (D&C 107:23). . . . So great is the sanctity of this special calling, that the title "Apostle" should not be used lightly as the common or ordinary form of address applied to living men called to this office. The quorum or council of the Twelve Apostles as existent in the Church today may better be spoken of as the "Quorum of the Twelve," the "Council of the Twelve," or simply as the "Twelve," than as the "Twelve Apostles," except as particular occasion may warrant the use of the more sacred term. It is advised that the title "Apostle" be not applied as a prefix to the name of any member of the Council of the Twelve; but that such a one be addressed or spoken of as "Brother—," or "Elder—," and when necessary or desirable, as in announcing his presence in a public assembly, an explanatory clause may be added, thus, "Elder—, one of the Council of the Twelve."[2]

THE FIRST PRESIDENCY AND QUORUM OF THE TWELVE

Concerning members of the First Presidency and the Quorum of the Twelve Apostles, President George Q. Cannon of the First Presidency bore this powerful testimony:

> Let me say to you—and I say it in the presence of the Great Eternal [God], before whom we shall all have to appear to answer for the deeds done in the body—that God has bestowed upon the First Presidency of this Church and upon the Apostles everything necessary to guide this people and to lead them back into the presence of God. I know that as I know that I live, and it is my testimony in your hearing today. There is no key, no authority, there is no revelation, there is no prophecy, there is nothing lacking. And though these men are earthen vessels, weak and fallible, yet God is with them, for He has chosen them.[3]

CALLED FOR A SPECIFIC WORK AND SERVICE

Regarding individuals who are called to serve in the leading councils of the Church, Elder Harold B. Lee spoke these insightful words:

> I heard the late [Elder] Orson F. Whitney, a member of the Twelve, deliver a very impressive sermon in the tabernacle prior to his passing. He moved his hand down over the pulpit below him where the General Authorities were sitting and said, "Now Brothers and Sisters, I don't think that these, my Brethren, are necessarily the best living men in the Church. I think there are other men who live just as good lives and maybe better lives than these General Authorities, but I'll tell you what I

do know, that when there's a vacancy in the ranks of the General Authorities, the Lord seeks out the man who is needed for a particular work and calls him to that service." He said, "I've watched that over the years."[4]

In conjunction with these expressions, the Prophet Joseph Smith stated, "We believe that a man must be called of God, by prophecy, and by the laying on of hands by those who are in authority, to preach the Gospel and administer in the ordinances thereof" (Articles of Faith 1:5).

Through his living prophet, the Lord calls each member of the Twelve for a particular work to do. Our Savior, Jesus Christ, knows each of us personally; therefore, He determines who will serve in the Quorum of the Twelve Apostles and the First Presidency. Truly, these Brethren are called by revelation and inspiration to serve in the leading councils of the Lord's only true and living Church, even The Church of Jesus Christ of Latter-day Saints. Our duty is to sustain them and follow their inspired teachings. For as our Savior has declared, "What I the Lord have spoken, I have spoken, and I excuse not myself . . . whether by mine own voice or by the voice of my servants, it is the same" (D&C 1:38).

VARIOUS MEMBERS OF THE TWELVE ARE RELATED TO OTHERS OF THE TWELVE

It is a known fact that various members of the Twelve are related to others of the Twelve. Some of this will be presented in this work. Concerning those who are related of the Jewish Twelve, the Nephite Twelve, and the Twelve called in this dispensation, see note 2 on pages 113–14 in Elder McConkie's *The Mortal Messiah: From Bethlehem to Calvary, Book 2*. After writing this excellent description, Elder McConkie concludes with these words: "Truly, faith runs in families, in all dispensations."[5]

STATISTICAL INFORMATION

- **Youngest Apostle not of the Quorum of the Twelve:** Joseph Smith, at age fourteen (*Joseph Smith–History* 1:3; 7).
- **Members of the Quorum of the Twelve Apostles ordained in this dispensation through 2005:** ninety-four.

- **Youngest man ordained to the Quorum of the Twelve Apostles:** Elder George A. Smith, at age twenty-one.[6]
- **Oldest member of the Quorum of the Twelve Apostles:** Elder George Q. Morris, at age eighty.[7]
- **Youngest man sustained as president of the Church:** Joseph Smith, at age twenty-six.[8]
- **Oldest man sustained as president of the Church:** Joseph Fielding Smith, at age ninety-three.[9]

Concerning This Work

Throughout this book, I have purposely limited my commentary, deferring to what members of the Twelve and First Presidency have said about their call to the apostleship. The Spirit will powerfully bear record that each Apostle is chosen by the Lord and revealed to the living prophet, who then ordains him. This well-documented and easy-to-read book provides a wealth of historical information about the apostleship—information that is finally brought together under one cover.

Acknowledgments

I am forever indebted to my wife, Brenda, for allowing me valuable time to research and write. I am appreciative of all of my family members—whose numbers happily keep increasing—for their constant love and support.

As I have written in my previous books, I am most appreciative to my dear friend, Dennis "C" Davis, who constantly shares his vast knowledge of the gospel with me and reviews my writings so that they will be doctrinally correct.

I am most grateful for my good friend Darrin Smith, of Hyrum, Utah, for furnishing various photographs that appear in this book.

CHAPTER 1

CALLING OF THE JEWISH TWELVE

Nearly a year and a half has passed since our Lord's mortal ministry began. The glorious day has finally arrived for establishing the foundation of the Church and kingdom of God on earth. The Son of God is going to call twelve men who will be his special witnesses; men who will bear, with Him, the burdens and responsibilities of the kingdom; men who will proclaim the saving truths of the gospel. Save Judas, the traitor, and John, the translated being, each will proclaim his apostolic testimony until his martyrdom.

These chosen individuals, says Elder McConkie, will be "Apostles of the Lord Jesus Christ—mighty men of faith; pillars of personal righteousness; chosen spirits who were before ordained to walk with Christ, teach his doctrine, and testify of his divine Sonship!"[1]

Those who preside in the leading councils of Christ's Church "must be called of God, by prophecy, and by the laying on of hands by those who are in authority, to preach the Gospel and administer in the ordinances thereof" (Articles of Faith 1:5).

Truly this is the Lord's work, and the Son of God knows whom He wants to serve in His Church. We visualize the Lord ascending a mountain to commune with His Father and God. In this secluded and quiet location, He earnestly seeks His Father's will concerning the Jewish Twelve. For as Jesus said at the Passover in Jerusalem, after healing the impotent man at the pool of Bethesda: "I can of mine own self do nothing . . . because I seek not mine own will, but the will of the Father which hath sent me" (John 5:30).

After their names were approved by the Father, we are told that "when it was day, he [Jesus] called unto him his disciples: and of them he chose twelve, whom also he named apostles" (Luke 6:13).

Again, Elder McConkie commented on this milestone moment in history. "The Twelve Apostles of the Lamb—the choicest and noblest spirits available to the God of Heaven to do his work in that day; the friends of his Son; those who shall see visions, receive revelations, and work wonders . . . What a glorious day this is in the cause of truth and righteousness!"[2]

PETER AND HIS FELLOW APOSTLES

Regarding Peter being the senior member of the Jewish Twelve, Elder James E. Talmage says:

> The three Gospel-writers who make record of the organization of the Twelve place Simon Peter first and Judas Iscariot last in the category; they agree also in the relative position of some but not of all the others. Following the order given by Mark, and this may be the most convenient since he names as the first three those who later became most prominent, we have the following list: Simon Peter, James (son of Zebedee), John (brother of the last-named), Andrew (brother of Simon Peter), Philip, Bartholomew (or Nathanael), Matthew, Thomas, James (son of Alpheus), Judas (also known as Lebbeus or Thaddeus), Simon (distinguished by his surname Zelotes, also known as the Canaanite), and Judas Iscariot.[3]

In addition to this description, Elder McConkie wrote, "There are reasons to believe that others of the original Twelve than Peter and Andrew [who were brothers, and], James and John [who also were brothers], were related, and that some of them were cousins of Jesus, but of these things we cannot be sure."[4]

Giving support "that some of them were cousins of Jesus," we turn to the time of our Savior's crucifixion. One reference reads, "Now there stood by the cross of Jesus his mother, and his mother's sister, Mary the wife of Cleophas, and Mary Magdalene" (John 19:25).

Regarding this scripture, Elder Talmage wrote:

> From the fact that John [the beloved Apostle] mentions the mother of Jesus and "his mother's sister" (John 19:25) and omits mention of Salome by name, some expositors [those individuals who expound or explain] hold that Salome was the sister of Mary the mother of Jesus; and therefore the Savior's aunt. This relationship would make James and John cousins to Jesus. While the scriptural record does not disprove this alleged kinship, it certainly does not affirm the same.[5]

Let us consider another point of view. Analyzing two New Testament scriptures that speak of the mother of Zebedee's children and the woman called Salome, the reader can formulate who was the mother of James and John.

Our attention is now turned to certain women who witnessed the death of our Savior on the cross.

First: "Among which was Mary Magdalene, and Mary the mother of James and Joses, and the mother of Zebedee's children" (Matthew 27:56).

Second: "There were also women looking on afar off: among whom was Mary Magdalene, and Mary the mother of James the less and of Joses, and Salome" (Mark 15:40).

In their separate work on the life of Christ, both Elders McConkie and Talmage quote from Jewish scholar Alfred Edersheim. As it pertains to Mary and her sister, Dr. Edersheim has written these declarative words, "Thus Salome, the wife of Zebedee and St. John's mother, was the sister of the Virgin, and the beloved disciple the cousin (on the mother's side) of Jesus, and the nephew of the Virgin. This also helps explain why the care of the Mother had been entrusted to him."[6]

In harmony with Dr. Edersheim's statement, Elder McConkie assuredly and without reservation says, "Jesus' attention is now turned to a scene of sorrow and despair. By the cross stands his mother. . . . With her are three other faithful women—her sister, Salome, the wife of Zebedee and the mother of James and John (who thus were cousins of Jesus), Mary the wife of Cleophas; and Mary Magdalene."[7]

Truly, believing blood flows in the veins of related brothers and cousins, who are called to be Apostolic witnesses of their Lord.

With this stated, we turn our attention to Peter, the senior Apostle. In less than two years, he will become the president of Christ's Church, following the crucifixion of our Lord. For the present, this mighty man of faith and action will be tutored and molded by the Master for the great leadership role he will assume.

The Savior explains to Peter and his fellow members of the Twelve, "Henceforth I call you not servants; for the servant knoweth not what his lord doeth: but I have called you friends; for all things that I have heard of my Father I have made known unto you." Then, He continues with these significant words, "Ye have not chosen me, but I have chosen you, and ordained you, that ye should go and bring forth fruit, and that your fruit should remain: that whatsoever ye shall ask of the Father in my name, he may give it you" (John 15:15–16).

From what is written in the Doctrine and Covenants, we know that Peter and his fellow Apostles became "special witnesses of the name of Christ" (D&C 107:23). In the near future, Jesus will give, first to Peter, James, and John and then to all the Twelve, the keys of the kingdom of heaven; these keys will enable them to preside over and "build up the church, and regulate all the affairs of the same" (D&C 107:33).

Shortly after the Jewish Twelve were ordained, the Son of God held a meeting and gave His special witnesses authority. What authority was given the Twelve? Our Lord gave them the priesthood, which allowed them to act in His name, teach the gospel, perform baptisms by immersion, cast out evil spirits, and heal all manner of sickness and all manner of disease. In addition, these mighty men of faith were given authority to raise the dead, as directed by the Spirit (see Matthew 10:1; Mark 6:7–13; Luke 9:1–6; John 4:1–3; JST John 4:2–4; and Acts 3:1–8; 9:36–42).

SIMON PETER TESTIFIED: "THOU ART THE CHRIST"

We now turn to a time when Jesus, in company with Peter and his fellow Apostles, travel northward to an area known as the "coasts of Caesarea Philippi" (Matthew 16:13; see also Mark 8:27). This is not a coastal area by a body of water, but as Elder Talmage explains, it is "an inland city situated near the eastern and principal source of the Jordan, and near the foot of Mount Hermon."[8]

From Luke, we are informed that when Jesus was "alone praying, his disciples were with him" (Luke 9:18). Based upon what is written, we may safely believe this is a private meeting, away from the masses of people who constantly seek the Lord's attention, a special meeting of sharing testimonies and receiving spiritual instruction. During the meeting, Jesus asks his disciples this searching question, "Who say the people that I am?" (JST Luke 9:18).

The men answer, "Some say, John the Baptist; but others say, Elias; and others, That one of the old prophets is risen again" (JST Luke 9:19).

Then our Lord specifically asks the Twelve, "But whom say ye that I am?" (Luke 9:20).

"Answering for all," Elder Talmage explains, "but more particularly testifying as to his own conviction, Peter, with all the fervor of his soul, voiced the great confession: 'Thou art the Christ, the Son of the living God' [Matthew 16:16; JST Mark 8:31]."[9]

This is not a new testimony but a fervent reaffirmation of that which this senior Apostle firmly believes and verbally declared on other occasions. For instance, following the sermon on the bread of life, when many disciples left and walked no more with our Lord, Jesus said unto the Twelve, "Will ye also go away?"

Simon Peter then answered, "Lord, to whom shall we go? thou hast the words of eternal life. And we believe and are sure that thou art that Christ, the Son of the living God" (John 6:67–69).

Returning to Peter's great declaration, Jesus speaks these words, "Blessed art thou, Simon Bar-jona: for flesh and blood hath not revealed it unto thee, but my Father which is in heaven" (Matthew 16:17).

Peter's birth name was Simon. At the time when Peter's brother Andrew introduced him to the Savior, Jesus said, "Thou art Simon the son of Jona: thou shalt be called *Cephas*, which is by interpretation, A stone" (John 1:42; emphasis added).

Describing what the Savior said to Peter, Elder Talmage has written this explanation, "The new name thus bestowed is the Aramaic or Syro-Chaldaic equivalent of the Greek 'Petros,' and of the present English 'Peter,' meaning 'a stone.'"[10]

From the Joseph Smith Translation of John, the following information is revealed: "And he [Andrew] brought him [Peter] to Jesus. And when Jesus beheld him [Peter], he said, Thou art Simon, the son of Jona, thou shalt be called Cephas, which is, by interpretation, a seer, or a stone" (JST John 1:42).

As mentioned previously, Jesus and His disciples are in Caesarea Philippi (located in northern Israel) near the base of Mount Hermon, an area with large boulders and rock formations. The melting snow that trickles down this mountain bubbles up underneath these huge stones.

This water then flows south into the Sea of Galilee and runs into the Jordan River. Water flowing from this "stone" is a type and symbol of the living water that will flow from the "stone of Israel" (Christ) to quench the thirst of Israel for the true word of God (see Genesis 49:24; 1 Peter 2:1–9; and D&C 50:44). Then, after His crucifixion, Jesus' words will be revealed to Peter—the senior Apostle and prophet and president of Christ's Church—whose name means "a seer, or a stone" (JST John 1:42).[11]

How fitting that both Christ's and Peter's name symbolize a stone, or most importantly a seer. For as has been written, "A seer is greater than a prophet. . . . A seer is a revelator and a prophet also; and a gift which is greater can no man have" (Mosiah 8:15–16).

The president of the Church holds the office of seership (see D&C 107:92; 124:94, 125). Indeed, the Apostolic office itself is one of seership, and the members of the Quorum of the Twelve Apostles, together with the Presidency of the Church, are chosen and sustained as prophets, seers, and revelators to the Church.

"And upon This Rock I Will Build My Church"

As soon as Simon finished bearing his great testimony, Jesus declares, "And I say also unto thee, That thou art Peter, and upon this rock I will build my church; and the gates of hell shall not prevail against it" (Matthew 16:18).

Upon what "rock" is Christ going to build His Church? Is it upon Peter, the rock and the seer?

The Prophet Joseph Smith revealed this great principle of truth. "And Jesus in His teaching says, 'Upon this rock I will build my Church, and the gates of hell shall not prevail against it.' What rock? Revelation."[12]

Therefore, we are plainly informed that Christ's true Church is not built upon Peter, the rock and seer, but upon the rock of revelation. Accordingly, Peter's great confession came by revelation, for as Jesus plainly says, "Blessed art thou, Simon Bar-Jona: for flesh and blood hath not revealed it unto thee, but my Father which is in heaven [by the power of the Holy Ghost]" (Matthew 16:17).

With this understanding, we continue with our Lord's words to His senior Apostle. "And I will give unto thee the keys of the kingdom of heaven: and whatsoever thou shalt bind on earth shall be bound in heaven: and whatsoever thou shalt loose on earth shall be loosed in heaven" (Matthew 16:19).

As Elder McConkie has aptly written:

> "The kingdom of heaven": the kingdom of God on earth; the Church of Jesus Christ organized among men; the earthly kingdom designated to prepare men for the heavenly kingdom of the Father—such is the meaning of the language of our Lord.
>
> "The keys of the kingdom": the governing, controlling, regulating power over the Church or kingdom; the instrumentality that opens the door to the receipt of peace in this life and eternal life in the world to come—such is what Jesus meant by keys.[13]

Through the Prophet Joseph Smith, the Lord has revealed this doctrine: "The keys of the kingdom . . . belong always unto the Presidency of the High Priesthood" (D&C 81:2), and only one man on earth, the president of the Church, can exercise them in their fulness (see D&C 132:7).

Bestowal of Keys

A week elapsed between the day Jesus promised to give the keys to Peter and that glorious day when the keys were actually conferred upon the three presiding Apostles (see Matthew 17:1; Mark 9:2; Luke 9:28). Mark [JST] says: "Jesus taketh Peter, and James, and John, who asked him many questions concerning his sayings; and Jesus leadeth them up into a high mountain apart by themselves" (JST Mark 9:1). Luke informs us that Jesus "took Peter and John and James, and went up into a mountain to pray" (Luke 9:28).

Probably it is the afternoon when these four ascend Mt. Hermon.[14] Once they reach their selected destination, they may have conversed for several hours about the Lord's sayings and the Lord would have done all He could to prepare these spiritual giants for the glorious experiences that would transpire in the evening.

Considering their climb up the mountain and the late hour of the night, it is natural for Peter, James, and John to be tired; in fact, the scriptures record these three are "heavy with sleep" (Luke 9:32). While they are sleeping, Jesus walks a short distance from them and prays to his Father. "And as he prayed, the fashion of his countenance was altered, and his raiment was white and glistering. And, behold, there talked with him two men, which were Moses and Elias [Elijah]: Who appeared in glory, and spake of his decease which he should accomplish at Jerusalem" (Luke 9:29–31).

Peter, James, and John are fully awakened from their deep sleep "by the surpassing splendor of the scene, and gazed with reverent awe upon their gloried Lord."[15] For as Peter later testified, these blessed men "were eyewitnesses of his majesty" (2 Peter 1:16).

"Spake of His Decease"

The King James Version of Luke says that Moses and Elijah "spake of his decease which he should accomplish at Jerusalem" (Luke 9:31). However, the Joseph Smith Translation reveals that Moses and Elijah "spake of his death, and also his resurrection, which he should accomplish at Jerusalem" (JST Luke 9:31). Though Jesus had previously told Peter and his fellow Apostles that he must go to Jerusalem "and be killed, and after three days rise again" (Matthew 16:21; see also Mark 8:31 and Luke 9:22), here upon the mount, these presiding Apostles are taught in plainness—from two translated prophets—of Christ's impending death and resurrection. This message, no doubt, helps these chosen men more fully know that Jesus will soon accomplish the mission which He came into the world to fulfill.

Peter, James, and John Were Transfigured

Concerning what transpired with these special witnesses, the Prophet Joseph Smith revealed, "The Priesthood is everlasting. The Savior, Moses, and Elijah, gave the keys to Peter, James, and John, on the mount, when they were transfigured before him."[16] It is important to emphasize that besides our Lord, the three presiding Apostles were also transfigured. "Transfiguration," explains Elder McConkie, "is a special change in appearance and nature which is wrought upon a person or thing by the power of God. This divine transformation is from a lower to a higher state; it results in a more exalted, impressive, and glorious condition."[17]

Moses and Elijah

Both Moses and Elijah spoke with Jesus. These ancient prophets were translated beings who had been taken into heaven without tasting death.

In the words of Elder McConkie, "These two joined with Jesus in conferring upon Peter, James, and John the keys of the kingdom."[18]

Moses restored the keys of the gathering of Israel and the leading of the Ten Tribes from the land of the north. Elijah restored the keys of the sealing power so that whatever Peter, James, and John bound or loosed on earth would be bound or loosed in heaven.

In our dispensation, Moses and Elijah conferred these same keys, by the laying on of hands, to Joseph Smith and Oliver Cowdery in the Kirtland Temple (see D&C 110:11–16).

JOHN THE BAPTIST

John the Baptist, who was beheaded by order of Herod the king (see Matthew 14:6–12; Mark 6:21–29; 9:7–9), also appeared on the Mount. "And there appeared unto them Elias with Moses, or in other words, John the Baptist and Moses; and they were talking with Jesus" (JST Mark 9:3).

Elder Talmage explains that "the authority of Elias is inferior to that of Elijah, the first being a function of the Lesser or Aaronic order of Priesthood, while the latter belongs to the Higher or Melchizedek Priesthood."[19]

Elder McConkie explains one reason for John's appearance, noting that "John the Baptist, a spirit personage whose mortal ministry completed what Moses had begun, was also present, rejoicing with his fellow laborers over the atonement about to be wrought."[20]

PRESIDING APOSTLES GIVEN ALL THEY NEEDED

In addition to the keys conferred by Moses and Elijah, Peter, James, and John received additional authority. Elder McConkie writes, "Jesus himself gave them all else that they needed to preside over his earthly kingdom; to lead all men to eternal salvation in the mansions on high; to send the gospel to the ends of the earth; and to seal men up unto eternal life in the kingdom of his Father."[21]

Concerning the presiding Apostles, our apostolic scholar asks and answers the following, "Why were these three repeatedly singled out and given special blessings and privileges? . . . By latter-day revelation we know that they held and restored 'the keys of the kingdom, which belong always unto the Presidency of the High Priesthood' (D&C 81:2), or in other words, they were the First Presidency in their day."[22]

There are other events that transpired on the mount that evening, but the most significant is this: Peter, James, and John received from Moses, Elijah, and Jesus all the keys and authority to preside over our Lord's earthly kingdom, following the Savior's death, resurrection, and ascension.

"TELL NO MAN"

We are not informed how long Jesus and His presiding Apostles were on the mountain. Evidently, they spent most of the night and part of the early morning enwrapped in the visions of eternity.

The Joseph Smith Translation of Mark says, "And as they came down from the mountain, he [Jesus] charged them that they should tell no man what things they had seen till the Son of Man was risen from the dead" (JST Mark 9:7). Not even their fellow Apostles were to know of the glorious events that transpired that sacred night. Evidently they were not yet prepared to understand or receive the wonderful truths that were revealed, in the words of Peter, upon the "holy mount" (2 Peter 1:18).

KEYS CONFERRED UPON THE REMAINING TWELVE

Jesus and the Jewish Twelve travel back to Capernaum. This town located on the western shore of the Sea of Galilee is designated as "his [Jesus'] own city" (Matthew 9:1; see also Mark 2:1). Elder McConkie further explains that "it was the home of Peter and Andrew, and of James and John, and that it was the place where Matthew sat as a collector of customs."[23]

While "in the house" of Peter, Jesus tells the Twelve, "Verily I say unto you, Whatsoever ye shall bind on earth shall be bound in heaven; and whatsoever ye shall loose on earth shall be loosed in heaven" (Matthew 8:5, 14; see also Matthew 18:18).

After our Lord and His presiding Apostles came down from the mountain, as Elder McConkie has explained, "sometime before these words were spoken in Capernaum; on some sacred, holy, and unnamed occasion, the remainder of the Twelve, all nine of them, received the keys of the kingdom of heaven. . . . Then he [Jesus] and the Three [Peter, James, and John]—acting, we may suppose, in concert—conferred those same keys and powers upon the others, all of whom (save Judas) used them for the salvation and exaltation of their fellowmen."[24]

APOSTOLIC SUCCESSION

On the shore of the Sea of Tiberias, which is also known as the Sea of Galilee and as the Sea or Lake of Gennesaret[25]—the resurrected Lord met and dined with seven members of the Jewish Twelve. Here, Peter gives his triple declaration of love. In addition, Jesus foretells of Peter's future martyrdom and of John becoming a translated being (see John 21:1–24).

"Throughout the forty days following His resurrection," says Elder Talmage, "the Lord manifested Himself at intervals to the Apostles, to some individually and to all as a body, and instructed them in 'the things pertaining to the kingdom of God.'"[26]

After witnessing the Lord's final ascension from the mount called Olivet, the eleven Apostles returned to Jerusalem. Our Apostolic scholar writes:

> The first official act undertaken by the Apostles was the filling of the vacancy in the council of the Twelve, occasioned by the apostasy and suicide of Judas Iscariot. . . . [by reason he was the President of the Church, and the senior Apostle] Peter laid the matter before the assembled Church. . . . Peter affirmed the necessity of completing the apostolic quorum; and he thus set forth the qualifications essential in the one who should be ordained to the Holy Apostleship. . . . Two faithful disciples were nominated by the Eleven, Joseph Barsabas and Matthias.[27]

Seeking divine guidance, the Apostles prayed to know the will of the Lord in the selection of the new Apostle. "And they gave forth their lots; and the lot fell upon Matthias" (Acts 1:26). Once again, the Twelve was fully organized. Though it is not written, we may safely believe that when the Apostles laid their hands on his head, Matthias was given the keys of the kingdom, the same keys that the other eleven held.

Elder Joseph Fielding Smith has written that "Paul was an ordained Apostle, and without question he took the place of one of the other brethren in that council."[28] (See also 1 Timothy 2: 1, 7; 2 Timothy 1:1, 11.)

As has been stated, Peter, James, and John were the First Presidency in their day.[29] Relying again upon Elder Smith for information, we read, "There is no evidence in any scripture or prophecy declaring that these three men acted independently, or apart from the Council of the Twelve Apostles. All the information we have indicates that they served in this capacity while serving at the same time as three of the Council of Twelve."[30]

Around A.D. 44, the first Herod Agrippa "stretched forth his hands to vex certain [individuals] of the church" and imprisoned Peter and "killed James the brother of John with the sword" (Acts 12:1–4).

Some scholars believe that this vacancy in the First Presidency was soon filled by another James, whom Paul says was the brother of Jesus. Concerning their individual callings as Apostles, Paul writes, "Neither went I up to Jerusalem to them which were Apostles before me; but I went into Arabia, and returned again unto Damascus. Then after three years I went up to Jerusalem to see Peter, and abode with him fifteen days. But other of the Apostles saw I none, save James the Lord's brother" (Galatians 1:17–19).

Other scriptures support the idea that this second James was a member of the First Presidency. Paul writes that "James, Cephas, and John . . . gave to me and Barnabas the right hands of fellowship; that we should go unto the heathen, and they unto the circumcision" (Galatians 2:9). As was explained earlier, Cephas is Peter's Aramaic name (see John 1:42).

John, who became a translated being, appears prominently with Peter in the first half of Acts. In the latter portion, James, the brother of the Lord, is the prominent leader in Jerusalem (see Acts 15:13; 21:18; see also Galatians 2: 9–12; 1 Corinthians 15:7). When an angel freed Peter from prison, the senior Apostle asked that word of his release be sent to "James, and to the brethren" (see Acts 12:17).

After his third missionary journey, Paul traveled to Jerusalem and visited with James. Paul followed the counsel of James to go to the temple and help weak members of the Church with their conversion process (see Acts 21:18–26).[31]

In addition, Luke tells us that Barnabas was an Apostle (see Acts 14:14). What we know of this man is that his name was Joses, or Joseph, and the Apostles gave him the surname of Barnabas. We further learn he was a Levite from the country of Cyprus, and he sold land and gave the money to the Apostles (see Acts 4:36–37). After Saul's conversion, Barnabas brought him to the Apostles and declared that he, Saul, had seen the Lord and had preached boldly of Christ at Damascus (see Acts 9:27). Later, the Apostles sent Barnabas to Antioch, where he and Saul, for a year, taught many people (see Acts 11:22–30; 12:25). Later, he and Paul (who formerly was Saul) were called to the ministry and sent forth to preach the gospel (see Acts 12–13, 15).

In writing of the ancient Apostles, Elder McConkie says, "Only Barnabas, Paul, Matthias, James the Lord's brother, and the original Twelve are singled out to carry the apostolic appellation."[32]

The ministry of the Apostles continued some sixty to seventy years from the time of the ascension of our Lord. Though the gospel was effectively taught by these special witnesses, the seed of apostasy had taken root in the Church. This condition was prophesized by Old Testament prophets, as well as the Lord himself (see Isaiah 24:1–6; Amos 8:11–12; Matthew 24:4–5, 10–13, 23–26).

Concerning this apostasy, the Lord said of the parable of the wheat and the tares, "Behold, verily I say, the field was the world, and the Apostles were the sowers of the seed; And after they have fallen asleep [meaning: died] the great persecutor of the church, the apostate . . . even Satan, sitteth to reign—behold he soweth the tares; wherefore, the tares choke the wheat and drive the church into the wilderness" (D&C 86:1–3).

Regarding the remaining member of the Jewish Twelve, Elder Talmage says, "The final ministry of John marked the close of the apostolic administration in the primitive Church. His fellow Apostles had gone to their rest, most of them having entered through the gates of martyrdom, and although it was his special privilege to tarry in the flesh until the Lord's advent in glory, he was not to continue his service as an acknowledged minister, known to and accepted by the Church."[33]

Through the long centuries of apostasy, John held the keys of the kingdom. Concerning this, we return to the exposition of the wheat and tares. "Therefore, thus saith the Lord unto you, with whom the priesthood hath continued through the lineage of your fathers" (D&C 86:8). However, it would not be until 1829 that Peter and James, as resurrected personages, and John, as a translated being, would appear to Joseph Smith and Oliver Cowdery. These ancient members of the First Presidency would confer upon their mortal fellows the Melchizedek Priesthood, the keys of the kingdom, and the keys of the dispensation of the fulness of times.[34]

CHAPTER 2

THE NEPHITE TWELVE

Concerning the appearance of the resurrected Lord to the Nephite multitude, we are informed that the storms, destruction, and darkness following the crucifixion of our Savior came to pass on the fourth day of the first month of the thirty-fourth year (see 3 Nephi 8:5). Then, "in the ending" of that same year, Jesus ministered personally among the Nephite people for many hours on several days (see 3 Nephi 10:18–19).

After Jesus introduced Himself to the multitude; after the multitude had all gone forth and thrust their hands into His side and felt the prints of the nails in His hands and feet; and after the multitude fell down and worshipped Him, the Savior spoke to Nephi and told him to come forth. Obediently, Nephi "arose and went forth, and bowed himself before the Lord and did kiss his feet" (3 Nephi 11:19)

This Nephi was entrusted with the plates of brass, and all the records and sacred items from his father, Nephi (see 3 Nephi 1:1–3). Concerning this righteous man, Dr. Sidney B. Sperry, a noted LDS scholar, has written this description:

> The powerful ministry of Nephi continued despite the sorrow and disappointment he must have suffered concerning the quick change of the Nephite people from righteousness to almost complete wickedness. His great spirituality is shown by the fact that he was blessed by the visitation of heavenly beings and by the voice of the Lord. (3 Nephi 7:15) With these great assurances, he went boldly among the people preaching repentance and remission of

sins through faith on the Lord Jesus Christ. His ministry was attended by such power and authority that Mormon says it would not suffice to write but part of certain things which he did (3 Nephi 7:17); therefore he did not write any of them in his book. The people were angry with him because his great power left them with no recourse. In the name of Jesus Christ he cast out devils and unclean spirits and healed the sick; he even raised his brother from death after the brother had been stoned by the people. Nephi converted a number of people by his preaching and baptized them unto repentance.[1]

Prior to the Jewish Twelve being called, Jesus prayed all night to know the will of His Father concerning those foreordained individuals. Now, having come from the presence of the Father, the resurrected Lord already knew the will of the Father, and He immediately called the Nephite Twelve.

With the multitude present, Christ told Nephi, "I give unto you power that ye shall baptize this people when I am again ascended into heaven" (3 Nephi 11:21). Not only was Nephi given this power, but the "Lord called others" (meaning eleven other righteous disciples) and gave them the same power (see 3 Nephi 11:22; 12:1).

"It may be asked why Nephi," says Dr. Sperry, "and possibly other members of the Twelve, had to receive authority to baptize (3 Nephi 11:22), and were themselves required to be baptized, when they had baptized many long years before the Savior's appearance (3 Nephi 7:23–26). The answer probably lies in the fact that when our Lord appeared to the Nephites, He proceeded to organize the Church in its fulness, and baptism under the Law of Moses was done away with."[2]

With another view, Elder Talmage says, "We read that before the second appearance of Christ to the Nephites, the chosen twelve were baptized (3 Nephi 19:10–13). These men had doubtless been baptized before, for Nephi had been empowered not only to baptize but to ordain others to the requisite authority for administering baptism (3 Nephi 7:23–26). The baptism of the disciples on the morn of the Savior's second visit, was in the nature of a rebaptism, involving a renewal of covenants, and confession of faith in the Lord Jesus."[3]

One important reason the Nephites were baptized again is a new dispensation of the gospel was introduced when Christ appeared.

Therefore, previous baptisms that had been performed under the Law of Moses were of no effect. Therefore, everything started over, and the ordinance of baptism into Christ's Church had to be administered again. (See 3 Nephi 15:2–10; see also D&C 22:1–4 concerning rebaptism in this dispensation.)

APOSTLES TO THE NEPHITES

Fortunately for us, Mormon wrote the names of the Nephite disciples: Nephi; Timothy, Nephi's brother, whom Nephi raised from the dead; Jonas, the son of Nephi; Mathoni; Mathonihah, the brother of Mathoni; Kumen; Kumenonhi; Jeremiah; Shemnon; Jonas; Zedekiah; and Isaiah (see 3 Nephi 19:4).

It is worth emphasizing that three members of Nephi's family were called by the resurrected Lord to serve in the Nephite Twelve—Nephi, his son, and his brother. In addition, two related brothers were also called. Once again, this demonstrates that believing blood runs in the veins of righteous families.

Concerning these twelve disciples, the Prophet Joseph Smith has written, "This book [the Book of Mormon] also tells us that our Savior made His appearance upon this [the American] continent after His resurrection; that He planted the Gospel here in all its fulness, and richness, and power, and blessing; that they had Apostles, Prophets, Pastors, Teachers, and Evangelists."[4]

Providing additional information, Elder Joseph Fielding Smith says, "While in every instance the Nephite Twelve are spoken of as disciples, the fact remains that they had been endowed with divine authority to be special witnesses for Christ among their own people. Therefore, they were virtually Apostles to the Nephite race, although their jurisdiction was, as revealed to Nephi, eventually to be subject to the authority and jurisdiction of Peter and the twelve chosen in Palestine."[5]

From these statements, we know that the Twelve Nephite disciples were actually Apostles, with a calling similar to the Jewish Twelve, who were chosen during our Lord's mortal ministry. Concerning the difference between the Jewish and Nephite Twelve, Dr. Sperry says, "It should be pointed out that although the Nephite Twelve were a quorum of Apostles and contemporary with the Twelve in Palestine, they were not *the* Quorum of the Twelve. The Twelve in Palestine must be given the honor. . . . In any question of ultimate authority, however academic, it must be admitted that the Twelve in Palestine had seniority over the Nephite Twelve."[6]

It may be asked why the Savior called the Jewish Twelve, as well as the Nephite Twelve. To find the answer, we turn to President Joseph F. Smith. He wrote, "It is true the Lord did appoint other Twelve upon this [American] continent, and His Church flourished and prospered in this land for many years, but the Lord declared that Peter, James, and John, and the Twelve that walked with Him at Jerusalem, held the Presidency over them. God may reveal himself to different nations, and establish among them the same Gospel and ordinances as He did anciently, if necessity require, but if these nations should be joined together there would be one head, and all the rest would be subordinate."[7]

In Mormon's abridgement of the calling of the Nephite Twelve, he briefly noted that the resurrected Lord said, "I give unto you power that ye shall baptize this people when I am again ascended into heaven" (see 3 Nephi 11:21). Fortunately for us, Moroni—the son of Mormon who was entrusted the sacred records—wrote this additional information, "The words of Christ, which he spake unto his disciples, the twelve whom he had chosen, as he laid his hands upon them—And he called them by name [individually], saying: Ye shall call on the Father in my name, in mighty prayer; and after ye have done this ye shall have power that to him upon whom ye shall lay your hands, ye shall give the Holy Ghost; and in my name shall ye give it, for thus do mine Apostles" (Moroni 2:1–2). Then, to emphasize his reason for writing this information, this last Nephite historian says, "Now Christ spake these words unto them at the time of his first appearing; and the multitude heard it not, but the disciples heard it; and on as many as they laid their hands, fell the Holy Ghost" (Moroni 2:3).

THE PRIESTHOOD OF THE NEPHITES

It is important to know that Alma, the father of Alma the younger, did not establish the Church of Jesus Christ among the Nephite people. Concerning this spiritual leader, we turn to Elder Joseph Fielding Smith for information. Elder Smith wrote, "While in the wilderness Alma organized his group of believers into a branch of the Church and is spoken of as their founder."[8]

Our Apostolic scholar further clarifies by saying, "The main body of the Nephites, under the second King Mosiah, was still intact in the land of Zarahemla. The reference stating that Alma was the founder of their church has reference only to the refugees who were fleeing from the land of the Nephites' first inheritance. In course of time they found their way back to the main body of the Church and Alma was consecrated as the high priest over the Church in all the lands occupied by the Nephites."[9] (See also Mosiah 18; 23:16–17.)

When the Savior appeared and called Nephi and his fellow disciples, they were already members of the Church. Further, they had baptized and ordained others to perform that ordinance many years before the Savior's appearance (see 3 Nephi 7:23–26).

Because the Nephite people were living the Law of Moses, it is proper to wonder whether they functioned under the Aaronic or the Melchizedek Priesthood. Elder Joseph Fielding Smith says, "The Nephites were descendants of Joseph. Lehi discovered this when reading the brass plates. He was a descendant of Manasseh, and Ishmael, who accompanied him with his family, was of the tribe of Ephraim. (Alma 10:3) Therefore there were no Levites who accompanied Lehi to the Western Hemisphere. Under these conditions the Nephites officiated by virtue of the Melchizedek Priesthood from the days of Lehi to the days of the appearance of our Savior among them."[10]

Shortly after the Jewish Twelve were ordained, the Son of God held a meeting and gave a distinctive authority to these, His special witnesses. On this important occasion, our Lord gave them the priesthood, which allowed them to act in His name, teaching the gospel, performing baptisms by immersion, casting out evil spirits, and healing all manner of sickness and disease. This authority was not given to the Nephite Twelve; as Elder Smith explained, they already held the Melchizedek Priesthood.

When the resurrected Lord appeared, He did away with the Law of Moses and told the multitude, "Marvel not that I said unto you that old things had passed away, and that all things had become new. Behold, I say unto you that the law is fulfilled that was given unto Moses. Behold, I am he that gave the law, and I am he who covenanted with my people Israel; therefore, the law in me is fulfilled, for I have come to fulfil the law; therefore it hath an end" (3 Nephi 15:3–5).

Now that the Law of Moses was fulfilled, the Nephite Twelve "were receiving a new commission," says Elder McConkie, "as part of a new dispensation. . . . Their commission, however, was to administer salvation to the Nephites in the Americas as contrasted with that of the Old World Twelve who were sent to all nations."[11]

Elder McConkie also noted that "they too had been taught true principles and were practicing true ordinances. And yet Jesus now renews and clarifies these policies and procedures among them, as we suppose he did also in Galilee."[12]

During His mortal ministry, Jesus—as the Good Shepherd—spoke these revealing words, "And other sheep I have, which are not of this fold: them also I must bring, and they shall hear my voice; and there shall be one fold, and one shepherd" (John 10:16).

Speaking to the Nephite Twelve, the Lord affirmed that never had the Father commanded Him to inform the Jews concerning the existence of the Nephites, except for mentioning indirectly other sheep not of the Jewish fold. Jesus plainly tells them they are the other sheep of whom He spoke of in Jerusalem (see 3 Nephi 15:14–24).

KEYS OF THE NEPHITE TWELVE

Through the ages, prophets and Apostles have held various keys. Nephi, the father of Nephi who was chosen as the head of the Nephite Twelve, was given the sealing power in his day (see Helaman 10:4–10).

We are not fully informed what keys the Nephite Twelve held. However, as Elder McConkie has explained, "The keys, as used in connection with priesthood and the Church and the kingdom, are the right of presidency; that is, they are the directing power, the ability to designate how and under what circumstances the priesthood will be used, and to regulate and govern all of the affairs of the church which is the kingdom."[13] Based on this statement, we may safely believe that because the Nephite Twelve held the priesthood and were chosen as Apostles to the Nephite people, they had the keys and authority to regulate and govern all of the affairs of the Church in their day.

DESIRES OF THE NEPHITE TWELVE

During His three-day ministry on the American continent, Jesus instituted the sacrament, spoke a marvelous prayer, and gave inspiring instructions. He healed all their sick and their lame, opened the eyes of their blind and unstopped the ears of the deaf, and did all manner of cures among them, even raising a man from the dead (see 3 Nephi 26:15). Children and "babes did open their mouths and utter marvelous things;

and the things which they did utter were forbidden that there should not any man write them" (3 Nephi 25:16).

From all that transpired during these three days, we may safely believe that the Nephite Twelve were highly enthused spiritually. Therefore, we turn our attention to the time when the Savior asked each of the Apostles this question: "What is it that ye desire of me, after that I am gone to the Father?" (3 Nephi 28:1).

Nine answered the Lord: "We desire that after we have lived unto the age of man, that our ministry, wherein thou has called us, may have an end, that we may speedily come unto thee in thy kingdom" (3 Nephi 28:2).

The Lord spoke this rewarding answer, "Blessed are ye because ye desired this thing of me; therefore, after that ye are seventy and two years old ye shall come unto me in my kingdom; and with me ye shall find rest" (3 Nephi 28:3).

We have no knowledge whether those nine died the year they turned seventy-two. Whenever this transpired, we can be assured that these faithful followers received the desired blessing from the Lord.

Jesus then "turned himself unto the three, and said unto them: What will ye that I should do unto you, when I am gone unto the Father?" Mormon reveals this insightful information: "And they sorrowed in their hearts, for they durst not speak unto him the thing which they desired" (3 Nephi 28:4–5).

The resurrected Lord told the three, "Behold, I know your thoughts and ye have desired the thing which John, my beloved, who was with me in my ministry, before that I was lifted up by the Jews, desired of me." Our Savior then declared, "Therefore, more blessed are ye [than the other nine Apostles] for ye shall never taste of death; but ye shall live to behold all the doings of the Father unto the children of men, even until all things shall be fulfilled according to the will of the Father, when I shall come in my glory with the powers of heaven" (3 Nephi 28:6–7).

Mormon records that Jesus touched each of the nine who were to live until they were seventy-two, but the three who were to tarry until he arrives in His glory, our Lord did not touch (3 Nephi 28:12).

Specifically speaking of the Three, Mormon says that a change came upon their bodies so that they could not die; in this state, they were to remain on the earth until the Second Coming of the Lord. At that time, they would undergo a greater change and be received into the kingdom of the Father. They were given a multitude of promises, including that they would suffer no pain or know sorrow, except for the sins of the world; that Satan was to have no power over them; and the powers of the earth could not hold them. (3 Nephi 28:36–40).

"Though they lived and labored as men among their fellows," says Elder Talmage, "preaching, baptizing, and conferring the Holy Ghost upon all who gave heed to their words, the enemies to the truth were powerless to do them injury. Somewhat later than a hundred and seventy years after the Lord's last visitation, malignant persecution was waged against the Three."[14]

Our Apostolic scholar continues, pointing out that "for nearly three hundred years, and possibly longer, the Three Nephites ministered visibly among their fellows; but as the wickedness of the people increased these special ministers were withdrawn, and thereafter manifested themselves only to the righteous few."[15]

We may be assured that nine of the Nephite Twelve passed on at their appointed time, and others were ordained in their place. The growth of the Church continued for a period of approximately one hundred and seventy years. Thereafter, pride entered into the hearts of the Nephite people, and they "began to be divided into classes; and they began to build up churches unto themselves to get gain, and began to deny the true church of Christ" (4 Nephi 1:25–26).

For many decades, violent wars were waged between the Lamanites and Nepites. This condition of animosity and apostasy continued until around 400 A.D. when the last great battle was fought near the Hill Cumorah. It was in this place, near Manchester, New York, that the Nephite nation sadly became extinct (see Mormon 1–9; see also Moroni 10).[16]

It would not be until the year 1829, when the Book of Mormon was translated by the Prophet Joseph Smith, that information concerning the Nephite Twelve would be known to the world. Concerning these chosen men, we conclude by repeating what Elder Joseph Fielding Smith wrote:

"While in every instance the Nephite Twelve are spoken of as disciples, the fact remains that they had been endowed with divine authority to be special witnesses for Christ among their own people. Therefore, they were virtually Apostles to the Nephite race, although their jurisdiction was, as revealed to Nephi, eventually to be subject to the authority and jurisdiction of Peter and the twelve chosen in Palestine."[17]

CHAPTER 3

HOW JOSEPH SMITH WAS AN APOSTLE

THE FIRST VISION

The foundation of The Church of Jesus Christ of Latter-day Saints is the story of the First Vision. Of all the mysteries of the gospel, this one has caused countless numbers of people to either decry it or testify of its truthfulness. Accordingly, it is the greatest truth or the greatest fraud.

JOSEPH SMITH

Joseph Smith was born December 23, 1805, at Sharon, Windsor County, Vermont. Having moved with his family near Palmyra, New York, Joseph states that in the spring of 1820, "I was at this time in my fifteenth year" (Joseph Smith–History 1:7), meaning, he was approaching his fifteenth birthday in December. "Some time in the second year after our removal to Manchester, there was in the place where we lived an unusual excitement on the subject of religion" (Joseph Smith–History 1:5).

> During this time of great excitement my mind was called up to serious reflection and great uneasiness; but though my feelings were deep and often poignant, still I kept myself aloof from all these parties, though I attended their several meetings as often as occasion would permit. . . .
>
> My mind at times was greatly excited, the cry and tumult were so great and incessant. . . .

23

> In the midst of this war of words and tumult of opinions, I often said to myself: What is to be done? Who of all these parties are right; or, are they all wrong together? If any one of them be right, which is it, and how shall I know it?
>
> I was one day reading the Epistle of James, first chapter and fifth verse, which reads: If any of you lack wisdom, let him ask of God, that giveth to all men liberally, and upbraideth not; and it shall be given him." (Joseph Smith–History 1:8–11)

Though these words have a universal application to all who seek to know the word of God, we discover, as Elder McConkie has written, that "yet they were preserved through the ages for the especial guidance of that prophet who should usher in the dispensation of the fulness of times."[1]

Continuing, Joseph says, "Never did any passage of scripture come with more power to the heart of man than this did. . . . I reflected on it again and again, knowing that if any person needed wisdom from God, I did" (Joseph Smith–History 1:12).

After seriously pondering this scripture, Joseph notes that "in accordance with this, my determination to ask of God, I retired to the woods to make the attempt. It was on the morning of a beautiful, clear day, early in the spring of eighteen hundred and twenty" (see Joseph Smith–History 1:14).

While in the woods, Joseph "kneeled down and began to offer up the desires of [his] heart to God." This young lad says, "I had scarcely done so, when immediately I was seized upon by some power which entirely overcame me, and had such an astonishing influence over me as to bind my tongue so that I could not speak. Thick darkness gathered around me, and it seemed to me for a time as if I were doomed to sudden destruction" (Joseph Smith–History 1:15).

"But, exerting all my powers to call upon God to deliver me out of the power of this enemy which had seized upon me, and at the very moment when I was ready to sink into despair and abandon myself to destruction—not to an imaginary ruin, but to the power of some actual being from the unseen world, who had such marvelous power as I had never before felt in any being" (Joseph Smith–History 1:16).

"I SAW TWO PERSONAGES"

The Prophet Joseph states that "just at this moment of great alarm, I saw a pillar of light exactly over my head, above the brightness of the sun, which descended gradually until it fell upon me" (Joseph Smith—History 1:16).

> It no sooner appeared than I found myself delivered from the enemy which held me bound. When the light rested upon me I saw two Personages, whose brightness and glory defy all description, standing above me in the air. One of them spake unto me, calling me by name and said, pointing to the other—"This is My Beloved Son. Hear Him!". . .
>
> I asked the Personages who stood above me in the light, which of all the sects was right (for at this time it had never entered into my heart that all were wrong)—and I should join.
>
> I was answered that I must join none of them, for they were all wrong; and the Personage who addressed me said that all their creeds were an abomination in his sight; that those professors were all corrupt; that: "they draw near to me with their lips, but their hearts are far from me, they teach for doctrines the commandments of men, having a form of godliness, but they deny the power thereof." (Joseph Smith–History 1:17–19)

Therefore, as Elder Joseph Fielding Smith has aptly explained, "After the vision was given to Joseph Smith of the Father and the Son, he stood as the only witness among men who could testify with knowledge that God lives and Jesus Christ is verily his Son. In this knowledge, he became a special witness for Christ and thus an Apostle before the Priesthood had been restored."[2]

THE TITLE *APOSTLE*

What does the title *Apostle* mean? Elder Joseph Fielding Smith says, "Men have been called Apostles who have been sent forth with the gospel message even when they have not been ordained to that particular office." He then quotes President Wilford Woodruff, saying, "'Let the Twelve

Apostles, and the Seventy Apostles, and High Priest Apostles and all other Apostles rise up and keep pace with the work of the Lord God, for we have no time to sleep.'"[3]

Continuing, Elder Smith says:

> To think that President Woodruff believed and intended to convey the thought that there were Apostles who were of the Twelve, and some of the seventies, and some of the high priests, is absurd. He merely desired to call attention to the fact that men holding these offices in the priesthood who were called to carry the gospel into the world as witnesses of its restoration should be alert and alive to their great responsibility.
>
> All men may, by virtue of the priesthood and the gift of the Holy Ghost, become witnesses for Christ . . . , but there is a special calling which is given to the Twelve special witnesses that separates them from other elders of the Church in the nature of their calling as witnesses. These Twelve men hold the fulness of authority, keys, and priesthood, to open up the way for the preaching of the gospel to every nation, kindred, and tongue.[4]

Elaborating further, Elder McConkie has written:

> This is the supreme office in the church in all dispensations because those so ordained hold both the fulness of the priesthood and all of the keys of the kingdom of God on earth. The President of the Church serves in that high and exalted position because he is the senior apostle of God on earth and thus can direct the manner in which all other apostles and priesthood holders use their priesthood. An apostle is an ordained office in the Melchizedek Priesthood, and those so ordained . . . are set apart as members of the Quorum of the Twelve and are given keys and power to preside over the church and kingdom and regulate all of the affairs of God on earth.
>
> Apostles are "special witnesses of the name of Christ in all the world." They are also "a Traveling Presiding High Council, to officiate in the name of the Lord, under

the direction of the Presidency of the Church, agreeable to the institution of heaven; to build up the church, and regulate all the affairs of the same in all nations, first unto the Gentiles and secondly unto the Jews." (D&C 107:23, 33)[5]

In a statement approved by the First Presidency, Elder James E. Talmage wrote, "The title 'Apostle' is one of special significance and sanctity; it has been given of God, and belongs only to those who have been called and ordained as 'special witnesses of the name of Christ in all the world, thus differing from other officers in the Church in the duties of their calling.' (Doc. and Cov. 107:23)."

Continuing, he says:

> So great is the sanctity of this special calling, that the title "Apostle" should not be used lightly as the common or ordinary form of address applied to living men called to this office. The quorum or council of the Twelve Apostles as existent in the Church to-day may better be spoken of as the "Quorum of the Twelve," the "Council of the Twelve," or simply as the "Twelve," than as the "Twelve Apostles," except as particular occasion may warrant the use of the more sacred term. It is advised that the title "Apostle" be not applied as a prefix to the name of any member of the Council of the Twelve; but that such a one be addressed or spoken of as "Brother—," or "Elder—," and when necessary or desirable, as in announcing his presence in a public assembly, an explanatory clause may be added, thus, Elder—, one of the Council of the Twelve.[6]

As it pertains to the Twelve selected in 1835, it is important to emphasize that under the direction of the First Presidency, the three witnesses were inspired by the Spirit of the Lord to choose the members of the Quorum of the Twelve. Therefore, these chosen and ordained men became "special witnesses of the name of Christ in all the world" (D&C 107:23).

How Joseph Was Able to See the Father and Son

Many people have wondered if the prophet saw the Father and the Son with his natural eyes or his spiritual eyes. To answer this question, we turn to Elder Spencer W. Kimball, who wrote:

> Moses declares "he saw God face to face, and he talked with him. . . ." (Moses 1:2).
>
> This experience with Moses is in harmony with the scripture that says:
>
> "For no man has seen God at any time in the flesh, except quickened by the Spirit of God.
>
> "Neither can any natural man abide the presence of God, neither after the carnal mind." (D&C 67:11–12)
>
> It must be obvious, then, that to endure the glory of the Father or the glorified Christ, a mortal being must be translated or otherwise fortified.
>
> Grease on the swimmer's body or a heavy rubber skin diver's suit may protect one from cold and wet; an asbestos suit might protect a firefighter from flames; a bullet-proof vest may save one from assassin's bullets; one's heated home may protect from winter's chilling blasts; deep shade or smoked glass can modify the withering heat and burning rays of the midday sun. There is a protective force that God brings into play when he exposes his human servants to the glories of his person and his works. . . . When properly protected with the glory of God, and when sufficiently perfected, man can see God.[7]

With another understanding, Elder Joseph Fielding Smith has written:

> We may after baptism and confirmation become companions of the Holy Ghost who will teach us the ways of the Lord, quicken our minds and help us to understand the truth. The people of the world do not receive the gift of the Holy Ghost.
>
> Joseph Smith did not have the gift of the Holy Ghost at the time of the First Vision, but he was overshadowed

by the Holy Ghost; otherwise, he could not have beheld the Father and the Son.[8]

In addition to being translated, or fortified with a protective force, or being overshadowed by the Holy Ghost, we discover another way that Joseph was able to see God. Regarding the higher or Melchizedek Priesthood, the Lord revealed the doctrine that "this greater priesthood administereth the gospel and holdeth the key of the mysteries of the kingdom, even the key of the knowledge of God. Therefore, in the ordinances thereof, the power of godliness is manifest. And without the ordinances thereof, and the authority of the priesthood, the power of godliness is not manifest unto men in the flesh; For without this no man can see the face of God, even the Father, and live" (D&C 84:19–22).

Based upon what is written in Doctrine and Covenants Section 84, various people have wondered how Joseph was able to see the Father and His Son in 1820, when he was not yet ordained to the Melchizedek Priesthood. To answer this question, we use the words of Elder Orson F. Whitney:

> It is said that without the Melchizedek Priesthood no man can look upon the face of God and live. And yet, Joseph Smith, when a boy of fourteen years, gazed upon the Father and the Son, and it was nine years before he held the Priesthood in the flesh. I once asked President Lorenzo Snow concerning this matter: "Why is it, if a man without the Melchizedek Priesthood cannot look upon God's face and live, that Joseph Smith could see the Father and the Son, and live, when he held no priesthood at all?" President Snow replied: "Joseph did hold the priesthood; he came with it into the world." I believed it before he said it, but I wanted him to say it first. Joseph Smith, as much as any Prophet that ever lived, was ordained a prophet before he came into this mortal life. He held the Melchizedek Priesthood in the spirit, when he came here [to earth], or he could never have received what he did from God.[9]

Then, in 1913, Elder Orson F. Whitney wrote:

> In view of the fact that these ordinations [to the Aaronic and Melchizedek Priesthoods] were subsequent

to the Prophet's vision, in the spring of 1820, when the Father and the Son appeared to him, some have found it difficult to interpret the divine declaration, that no man without the Melchizedek Priesthood "can see the face of God, even the Father, and live" (D&C 84:19–22). But the problem is easy of solution, in the light of the Prophet's teachings. Did he not give the key to it when he said that certain men, called to minister to the inhabitants of this world, were ordained to that very purpose before the world was?

For if no man without the Melchizedek Priesthood can see the face of God the Father and live, and Joseph Smith, nine years before he received either of the Priesthoods from those heavenly messengers, looked upon the faces of both the Father and the Son and survived, it indicates, in accordance with his own statement . . . that certain spirits are ordained to certain callings before they tabernacle in the flesh, and that he himself held the Melchizedek Priesthood when he saw the face of God at the opening of the last gospel dispensation.[10]

In a personal letter dated February 20, 1881, Joseph F. Smith, a member of the First Presidency at the time, wrote, "Joseph Smith held the Melchizedek Priesthood before he came to the earth—as did Jesus—but it had to be reconfirmed upon him in the flesh by Peter, James and John, as upon Jesus by Moses and Elias on the Mount."[11]

Also in a personal letter, which was dated January 3, 1947, Elder Joseph Fielding Smith wrote that "President Lorenzo Snow said that Joseph Smith could see God because of the power of the Priesthood which he held before he came here. Without any doubt men chosen to positions of trust in the spirit world, held priesthood."[12]

From what we read, we discover that there are at least three ways in which Joseph Smith was able to see the Father and the Son. Now, it is important to emphasize that the Father and the Son can appear to anyone, including women, who are not foreordained to the priesthood. Another view regarding the statement in Doctrine & Covenants 84 is that without the blessings of the Melchizedek Priesthood, particularly temple ordinances, it is impossible for men or women to "dwell" or "see" God in the next life.

Regarding Joseph Smith seeing the Father and the Son, we repeat what Elder Joseph Fielding Smith wrote, "After the vision was given to Joseph Smith of the Father and the Son, he stood as the only witness among men who could testify with knowledge that God lives and Jesus Christ is verily his Son. In this knowledge he became a special witness for Christ, and thus an Apostle before the Priesthood had been restored."[13]

APPEARANCE OF JOHN THE BAPTIST

Our attention is now turned to 1829. While translating the Book of Mormon, Joseph Smith and Oliver Cowdery, his scribe, discovered that the question of baptism for the remission of sins was written several times in the ancient record. Because the doctrine of baptism was misunderstood at the time, these references caused Joseph and Oliver to marvel. After discussing the subject, they decided to inquire of the Lord for knowledge.

On May 15, 1829, they retired to the woods and prayed for instruction. While engaged in prayer, a heavenly messenger descended in a cloud of light and introduced himself as John the Baptist from the New Testament. He told these men that he acted under the direction of Peter, James, and John, who held the keys of the Melchizedek Priesthood, and that he had been sent to confer upon Joseph and Oliver the Aaronic Priesthood, which holds the keys of the temporal gospel. After placing his hands upon their heads, this heavenly personage said, "Upon you my fellow servants, in the name of Messiah I confer the Priesthood of Aaron, which holds the keys of the ministering of angels, and of the gospel of repentance, and of baptism by immersion for the remission of sins; and this shall never be taken again from the earth, until the sons of Levi do offer again an offering unto the Lord in righteousness"(D&C 13).[14]

Under John the Baptist's direction, Joseph first baptized Oliver and then Oliver baptized Joseph. Now, for the first time in several centuries, there were men with priesthood authority to officiate in baptism for the remission of sin.[15]

APPEARANCE OF PETER, JAMES, AND JOHN

It is important to know that in the dispensation of the fulness of times—which is the dispensation we are in now—"a whole and complete and perfect union, and welding together of dispensations, and keys, and powers, and glories should take place, and be revealed from the days of Adam even to the present time" (D&C 128:18).

Note these words, "The voice of Peter, James, and John in the wilderness between Harmony, Susquehanna county, and Colesville, Broome county, on the Susquehanna river, declaring themselves as possessing the keys of the kingdom, and of the dispensation of the fulness of times!" (D&C 128:20).

And the Prophet Joseph declares, "The voice of Michael, the archangel; the voice of Gabriel, and of Raphael, and of divers angels, from Michael or Adam down to the present time, all declaring their dispensation, their rights, their keys, their honors, their majesty and glory, and the power of their priesthood; giving line upon line, precept upon precept; here a little, and there a little" (D&C 128:21).

In another revelation, the Lord declares that He shall partake of the sacrament with Joseph Smith and Oliver Cowdery in His kingdom, and also with John, who ordained them to the "first priesthood" (see D&C 27:7–8). Then these informative words are written, "And also with Peter, and James, and John, whom I have sent unto you, by whom I have ordained you and confirmed you to be Apostles, and especial witnesses of my name" (D&C 27:12).

Thus the Lord declares that Joseph and Oliver were ordained by Peter, James, and John. Therefore, the priesthood with its keys existed before the Church was officially organized on April 6, 1830.

Joseph and Oliver: Special Witnesses

Elder Joseph Fielding Smith provides this insight:

> In the Doctrine and Covenants, section 27:12–13, the Lord says that he sent Peter, James, and John to ordain Joseph Smith and Oliver Cowdery and that by virtue of that ordination they became Apostles and special witnesses. This is true, but . . . these men were not ordained to the specific office in the priesthood, but received the priesthood itself out of which the offices come. Joseph Smith and Oliver Cowdery were therefore, by virtue of the conferring of priesthood, Apostles or special witnesses, for Jesus Christ.[16]

This doctrine was previously taught to Elder Smith from his father, President Joseph F. Smith, then of the First Presidency:

> It was the Melchizedek Priesthood that was conferred

upon Joseph Smith and Oliver Cowdery by Peter, James and John. Neither of them was ordained to any office in that priesthood by the messengers, but that priesthood holds the keys to all the offices in the church, and until the church was organized and offices in the priesthood became necessary there were no offices conferred . . . the office derives its authority from the priesthood. The Prophet held all the priesthood which he received under the hands of the angels, but none of the offices growing out of it until they were subsequently bestowed upon him by the Church.[17]

Armed with this information, Elder Joseph Fielding Smith wrote these declarative words: "These men were not ordained to the special calling, or office, as Apostles. . . . In a similar manner Peter, James, and John conferred upon them [Joseph and Oliver] the Melchizedek Priesthood, and not an office. . . . Having received the priesthood, they had power to ordain each other, after the organization of the Church, to offices in this priesthood, for the Lord had said that all offices are appendages of the priesthood and grow out of it" (D&C 84:29–30; see also 107:5).[18]

In harmony with this statement, President Brigham Young says, "Brother Joseph [Smith] received the Patriarchal or Melchizedek Priesthood from under the hands of Peter, James, and John. From those Apostles Joseph received every power, blessing, and privilege of the highest authority of the Melchizedek Priesthood ever committed to man on the earth."[19]

Concerning the appearance of the ancient First Presidency, Elder McConkie wrote:

Soon thereafter Peter and James, in resurrected glory, and John their fellow minister, serving as a translated being, came also to Joseph Smith and Oliver Cowdery. These heavenly ministrants conferred upon their mortal fellows the Melchizedek Priesthood, the keys of the kingdom of God, and the keys of the dispensation of the fulness of times (D&C 27: 12–13). This higher priesthood embraces within it the holy Apostleship and is the power by which the gospel and the Church are administered. . . . Being thus empowered from on high, the recipients of so great a boon were able to organize the church and kingdom of God on earth, which they did on 6th of April in 1830.[20]

Therefore, as Elder Joseph Fielding Smith wrote, "On the day of the organization of the Church, Joseph Smith ordained Oliver Cowdery to the office of elder, and Oliver Cowdery ordained Joseph Smith to that same office, in keeping with the instructions they had received from the heavenly messengers who had first come to them. . . . When the Church was organized, Joseph Smith and Oliver Cowdery received the first offices coming out of the priesthood and bestowed for the necessary government of the Church."[21]

In harmony with this doctrine, Elder McConkie wrote, "In fact, Joseph Smith became an apostle in the spring of 1820, as a result of the First Vision, even before priesthood was conferred upon him through the ministration of Peter, James, and John; and after the Church was established, the Lord ordained (*meaning decreed*) that he continue to serve in this high apostolic station (D&C 20:1–4; 21:1; 27:12)."[22]

It is important to note the following ordinations and callings of the Prophet Joseph Smith:

1. Early in the spring of 1820: At the appearance of God the Father and His Son, Jesus Christ, Joseph Smith, at age fourteen, became an Apostle before the priesthood was restored (see Joseph Smith–History 1:17–20).
2. May 15, 1829: John the Baptist appeared and conferred the Aaronic Priesthood on Joseph Smith, age twenty-three; he then was baptized (see D&C 13).[23]
3. May or June 1829: Peter, James, and John appeared and conferred the Melchizedek Priesthood, the keys of the kingdom of God, and the keys of the dispensation of the fulness of times on Joseph Smith at age twenty-three. This higher priesthood embraces within it the holy Apostleship (see D&C 27:12–13; 128:20).[24]
4. April 6, 1830: On the day the Church was organized, Joseph Smith, at age twenty-four, was ordained and sustained as the first elder of the Church.[25]
5. April 6, 1830: The Lord says of Joseph Smith, "Behold, there shall be a record kept among you; and in it thou shalt be called a seer, a translator, a prophe*t*, an apostle of

Jesus Christ, an elder of the church through the will of God the Father, and the grace of your Lord Jesus Christ" (D&C 21:1).

6. June 3, 1831: Joseph Smith, age twenty-five, was ordained a high priest by Lyman Wight.[26]
7. January 25, 1832: Joseph Smith, at age twenty-six, was ordained President of the High Priesthood at a conference at Amherst, Ohio.[27]

Thus, the Lord chose in the first place an Apostle, Joseph Smith, to commence the building up of the kingdom of God, and He did not organize the Church until he first received the priesthood. Then, under His direction, the Quorum of the Twelve Apostles was called and ordained. From this information, we see that Joseph Smith was an Apostle. Though he never served as an ordained member of the Quorum of the Twelve Apostles, Joseph Smith was the first Apostle in this dispensation.

CHAPTER 4

THE QUORUM OF THE TWELVE APOSTLES

THE THREE WITNESSES CHOSE THE TWELVE

As early as June 1829, a revelation instructed the witnesses to the Book of Mormon [Oliver Cowdery, David Whitmer, and Martin Harris] to "search out the Twelve." In this revelation, the Lord made known His purpose to select Twelve Apostles: these individuals must take upon them the name of Christ, with full purpose of heart, and be prepared to go to all parts of the world and preach the gospel to every creature (D&C 18:26–39).

It would be nearly six years later before the Twelve were actually chosen. On Sunday, February 8, 1835, the Prophet Joseph called Brigham Young and Brigham's brother, Joseph, to his residence in Kirtland, Ohio. Of this meeting, President Young relates said, "We went and sung to him a long time, and talked with him. He then opened the subject of the Twelve and Seventies for the first time I ever thought of it. He said, 'Brethren, I am going to call out Twelve Apostles . . . and select a Quorum of Seventies from those who have been up to Zion, out of the camp boys.'"[1]

ORSON PRATT

Providing further information, Brother Joseph Young records what the Prophet told his brother, Brigham: "'I wish you to notify all the brethren living in the branches, within a reasonable distance from this place, to meet at a general conference on Saturday next. I shall then and there appoint twelve Special Witnesses, to open the door of

37

the Gospel to foreign nations, and you,' said he (speaking to Brother Brigham), 'will be one of them.' He [the Prophet] then proceeded to enlarge upon the duties of their calling. The interest that was taken on the occasion of this announcement produced in the minds of the two Elders present a great sensation and many reflections. . . . Agreeable to his request to Elder Brigham Young, the branches were all notified, and a meeting of the brethren in general conference was held in Kirtland, in the new school house under the printing office, on the following Saturday, February 14th."[2]

At this special conference, President Joseph Smith reported that the meeting had been called because God had commanded it. The Prophet further stated that this information was made known to him by vision and by the Holy Spirit. After an opening prayer, President Smith noted that the first item of business was for the Three Witnesses of the Book of Mormon to pray individually, and then proceed to choose twelve men as Apostles. Following these prayers, the First Presidency—Presidents Joseph Smith, Sidney Rigdon, and Frederick G. Williams[3]—laid their hands on the heads of the witnesses and blessed them. The three witnesses began to choose the Twelve, and these men were chosen in the following order:

1. Lyman E. Johnson
2. Brigham Young
3. Heber C. Kimball
4. Orson Hyde
5. David W. Patten
6. Luke S. Johnson
7. William E. McLellin[4]
8. John F. Boynton
9. Orson Pratt
10. William Smith
11. Thomas B. Marsh
12. Parley P. Pratt[5]

Elder Joseph Fielding Smith summarized the ordination of the Apostles by the three witnesses. He wrote:

> Lyman E. Johnson, Brigham Young, and Heber C. Kimball were then called forward, ordained, and instructed in that order, after which the meeting

adjourned. The following day, February 15th, the ordinations continued. Orson Hyde, David W. Patten and Luke S. Johnson were called forward and ordained. William E. McLellin, John F. Boynton and William Smith [the Prophet's brother[6]] were also each ordained after which the congregation adjourned. Some of the brethren were absent on this occasion. February 21, 1835, Parley P. Pratt was ordained. Elders Thomas B. Marsh and Orson Pratt [the brother of Parley], being away on missions, it was not until near the end of April when they were ordained. Elder Marsh returned to Kirtland, April 25th, and Elder Orson Pratt on the following day.[7]

Concerning the first three called to receive ordination, Elder Heber C. Kimball provides this added, interesting information: "After we had thus been ordained by these brethren [Three Witnesses], the First Presidency laid their hands on us and confirmed these blessings and ordinations, and likewise predicted many things which should come to pass."[8]

Later, these Twelve Apostles were organized according to age as follows:

1. Thomas B. Marsh, age 35
2. David W. Patten, age 35
3. Brigham Young, age 33
4. Heber C. Kimball, age 33
5. Orson Hyde, age 30
6. William E. McLellin, age 29
7. Parley P. Pratt, age 27
8. Luke S. Johnson, age 27
9. William Smith, age 23
10. Orson Pratt, age 23
11. John F. Boynton, age 23
12. Lyman E. Johnson, age 23[9]

Concerning the witnesses choosing and ordaining the Twelve, President Joseph F. Smith said:

> Witness the calling, on February 14, 1835, of David Whitmer and Martin Harris, both high priests, by the Prophet Joseph Smith, in conformity with prior revelation

from God (see Doctrine and Covenants, section 18) to "search out the Twelve." They chose the Twelve, ordained and set them apart for their exalted callings, because they were called upon by the prophet of God who had been instructed of the Lord, and also because these men held the necessary authority of the Priesthood, which authority was exercised, in this case, as it should be in all cases, upon proper calling.[10]

As far as the selection of the Twelve in 1835, we should emphasize that under the direction of the First Presidency, the Three Witnesses were inspired by the Spirit of the Lord to choose the members of the Quorum of the Twelve. Therefore, these chosen and ordained men became "special witnesses of the name of Christ in all the world" (D&C 107:23).

A general charge to the Twelve was given by President Oliver Cowdery. At the conclusion of this charge, he took them separately by the hand and said, "Do you with full purpose of heart take part in this ministry, to proclaim the Gospel with all diligence, with these your brethren, according to the tenor and intent of the charge you have received?"[11] Each answered in the affirmative. In his autobiography, Elder Parley P. Pratt refers to this question put to each of the Twelve by Elder Cowdery as the "Oath and Covenant of the Apostleship."[12]

IMPORTANT INSTRUCTION

On February 27, 1835, nine of the twelve—Lyman Johnson, Brigham Young, Heber C. Kimball, Orson Hyde, David W. Patten, Luke Johnson, William E. McLellin, John F. Boynton, and William Smith—assembled at the home of President Joseph Smith. President Smith was present with his two counselors, Frederick G. Williams and Sidney Rigdon. Bishop Newel K. Whitney was present with three elders. Parley P. Pratt had gone to New Partage, and Orson Pratt and Thomas B. Marsh had not yet received their ordination.

After President Smith opened by prayer, he said he had something of importance to lay before the council:

> Since the Twelve are now chosen, I wish to tell them a course which they may pursue and be benefited hereafter in a point of light of which they, perhaps, are not now aware. At all times when you assemble in the

capacity of a council to transact business . . . let one or more be appointed to keep a record of your proceedings and on the decision of every important item, be it what it may, let such decision be noted down, and they will ever remain upon record as law, covenant and doctrine. Questions thus decided might at the time appear unimportant, but . . . afterward, you might find them of infinite worth not only to your brethren but a feast also to your own souls. . . .

Now in consequence of a neglect to write these things when God reveals them—not esteeming them of sufficient worth—the spirit may withdraw and God may be angry and here is a fountain of intelligence or knowledge of infinite importance which is lost. . . . Now if you will be careful to keep minutes of these things as I have said, it will be one of the most important and interesting records ever seen. I have now laid these things before you for your consideration and you are left to act according to your own judgment."[13]

After seriously considering the Prophet's instruction, the members of the council appointed Elders Orson Hyde and William E. McClellin as clerks of the meeting.[14] A record of their meetings has been kept from February 27, 1835, to our present day.

Supporting this statement, Elder Joseph Anderson, then an assistant to the Twelve, said, "I've had the opportunity of reading the minutes of the Council of the First Presidency and the Quorum of the Twelve, back to the days of Brigham Young. In these minutes are recorded revelations that were given to these men during their administration. They contain the testimonies that were given concerning the Prophet Joseph Smith, and others."[15]

On March 12, 1835, the Twelve met in council and were appointed by the First Presidency to a mission; the men were charged with visiting the branches throughout the Eastern States and regulating the affairs of the Church. Minutes note that those in attendance unanimously agreed that the Twelve leave Kirtland on May 4, 1835.

During this particular mission, Elder Brigham Young was specifically instructed to open the door of the gospel to remnants of Joseph (the American Indian); this motion was carried. On March 28, 1835, the

Twelve asked the Prophet for a blessing by way of revelation. Following this request, President Smith inquired of the Lord and received what is called the great revelation on Priesthood, Doctrine and Covenants Section 107. In this section, the various offices and the powers pertaining to each are fully explained. In addition, the Lord notes that the First Presidency, the Twelve, and the Seventy constitute the presiding quorums of the Church. Further, the Twelve are to set in order the officers of the Church. As agreed, the members of the Twelve left Kirtland on the morning of May 4, 1835, for their respective missions.[16]

First Official Statement by the Twelve

On September 24, 1834, a general assembly of Latter-day Saints appointed a committee—consisting of Joseph Smith, Sidney Rigdon, Oliver Cowdery, and Frederick G. Williams—for the purpose of arranging the Revelations received so far from the Lord. The committee completed this assignment, and on August 17, 1835, the work was presented to a general assembly at Kirtland under the name the Book of Doctrine and Covenants of the Church; the assembly accepted the compilation by unanimous vote.

President William W. Phelps read the written testimony of the Twelve, which evidently was prepared before their departure for their first mission. The following statement is also written in modern editions of the Doctrine and Covenants:

> ### TESTIMONY OF THE TWELVE APOSTLES TO THE TRUTH OF THE BOOK OF DOCTRINE AND COVENANTS
>
> *The Testimony of the Witnesses to the Book of the Lord's Commandments, which commandments He gave to His Church through Joseph Smith Jun., who was appointed by the voice of the Church for this purpose:*
>
> We, therefore, feel willing to bear testimony to all the world of mankind, to every creature upon the face of the earth, that the Lord has borne record to our souls, through the Holy Ghost shed forth upon us, that these commandments were given by inspiration of God, and are profitable for all men and are verily true.
>
> We give this testimony unto the world, the Lord being

our helper; and is through the grace of God the Father, and His Son, Jesus Christ, that we are permitted to have this privilege of bearing this testimony unto the world, in the which we rejoice exceedingly, praying the Lord always that the children of men may be profited thereby.

The names of the Twelve were:

Thomas B. Marsh	David W. Patten
Brigham Young	Heber C. Kimball
Orson Hyde	Wm. E. McLellin
Parley P. Pratt	Luke S. Johnson
William Smith	Orson Pratt
John F. Boynton	Lyman E. Johnson[17]

This is the first official statement written by the Quorum of the Twelve in this dispensation following their ordination as Apostles.

From this point forward, this book will not follow a chronological order of events that transpired in the lives of the Twelve. It will, however, present dates and insightful information concerning those called to be Apostles. Elder Joseph Fielding Smith said:

> There is no set rule in regard to the choosing of apostles. For instance: The first Twelve chosen in this dispensation were selected by the Three Witnesses. Others, both in the day of the Prophet and since his day, have been chosen by direct revelation through the President of the Church. Others have been chosen as was Matthias in the days of the ancient apostles. At other times, the members of the Presidency and the Twelve present names which are considered by the First Presidency and one chosen by "lot" much as Matthias was.[18]

Kirtland Temple (Above)

Interior of Kirtland Temple (Below)

CHAPTER 5

THE TWELVE AND THE KIRTLAND TEMPLE

On the evening of October 5, 1835, the Prophet met in a council meeting of the Twelve and gave them instruction concerning their duties. President Smith told the Twelve it was the will of God that they were to take their families and move to the state of Missouri the following summer with the presidency. And, this fall, the Prophet noted, they were to attend to the ordinance of washing of feet; and prepare for an endowment [in the Kirtland Temple].[1]

Less than a month later, on Tuesday, November 3, the word of the Lord came to the Prophet concerning the Twelve. Though a record of this revelation is not included in the *Doctrine and Covenants*, it is recorded and is titled a Revelation to the Twelve:

> Behold they are under condemnation, because they have not been sufficiently humble in my sight, and in consequence of their covetous desires, in that they have not dealt equally with each other in the division of the monies which came into their hands, [With a qualifying statement, the Lord says:] nevertheless, some of them dealt equally, therefore they shall be rewarded; but verily I say unto you [Joseph], they must all humble themselves before me, before they will be accounted worthy to receive an endowment [in the Kirtland Temple], to go forth in my name unto all nations. . . . I appoint these Twelve that they should be equal in their ministry, and in their portion, and in their evangelical rights . . . and

prepare their hearts for the solemn assembly, and for the great day which is to come, verily thus saith the Lord. Amen.[2]

Though we are not fully informed how members of the Twelve were notified of this revelation, the Prophet writes that Elders William E. McLellin and Orson Hyde desired to hear what the Lord said. The Prophet had his scribe read it to them. After examining their own hearts, these two men acknowledged that the revelation came from the Lord and expressed their satisfaction with it. Later that day, Elder Brigham Young had the revelation read to him, and he too appeared perfectly satisfied with what it said. Nothing is written of the reaction of the other members of the Twelve at that time. We may safely believe that they also acknowledged this revelation was from the Lord and was for their benefit.[3]

Work on the Kirtland Temple was nearing completion. Leading councils of the Church greatly anticipated the privilege of entering into the house of the Lord. On Thursday, November 12, 1835, the Prophet met with nine members of the Twelve and told them that in order to make the foundation of the Church complete, they needed the ordinances of the washing of feet and the endowment, which would be performed in the temple. At the conclusion of his remarks, President Smith stated that all who were prepared to abide the presence of the Savior would see Him in the solemn assembly.[4]

On Thursday, January 21, 1836, the first meeting was held in the newly completed Kirtland Temple. While here, the Prophet received various visions. One is recorded in D&C 137. In another, President Smith saw the Twelve Apostles standing together in a circle, fatigued, with their clothes tattered, their feet swollen, and their eyes downward. In their midst was the Savior, but they did not see Him. Looking at the Twelve, Jesus wept.[5]

Concerning this particular vision, Elder Heber C. Kimball provided this added, fascinating information:

> During this time many great and marvelous visions were seen, one of which I will mention which Joseph the Prophet had concerning the Twelve. His anxiety was and had been very great for their welfare, when the following vision was manifested to him, as near as I can recollect:

He saw the Twelve going forth, and they appeared to be in a far distant land. After some time they unexpectedly met together, apparently in great tribulation, their clothes all ragged, and their knees and feet sore. They formed in a circle, and all stood with their eyes fixed upon the ground. The Savior appeared and stood in their midst and wept over them, and wanted to show Himself to them, but they did not discover Him. He (Joseph) saw until they had accomplished their work, and arrived at the gate of the celestial city; there Father Adam stood and opened the gate to them, and as they entered he embraced them one by one and kissed them. He then led them to the throne of God, and then the Savior embraced each one of them and kissed them, and crowned each one of them in the presence of God. [It is important to note these words:] He saw that they all had beautiful heads of hair and all looked alike. The impression this vision left on Brother Joseph's mind was of so acute a nature, that he never could refrain from weeping while rehearsing it.[6]

Regarding the members of the Quorum of the Twelve in this dispensation looking alike, it is proper to wonder if this refers to their physical appearance or the equally brilliant spiritual brightness, which they radiated, a brightness that Lehi glimpsed in his vision of the Jewish Twelve (see 1 Nephi 1:10). We trust that someday we can receive a definitive answer to this intriguing statement.

The Prophet also saw in vision Elder McLellin preaching to a vast multitude of people in the south. By Elder McLellin's word and the power of God, a lame man threw his crutches down and leaped about. In addition, the Prophet saw Elder Brigham Young preaching in the desert to a dozen Indian men, who appeared hostile. He was preaching to them in their native tongue, an angel of God standing above his head with a drawn sword, protecting him; Elder Young did not see him.

President Smith then says that he saw the Twelve in the celestial kingdom of God. More will be written of this later in this work, but six of the first Twelve Apostles were excommunicated. Whether the Prophet is referring to the first members of the Twelve, we are left to wonder.[7]

On the evening of Friday, January 22, 1836, the First Presidency met with the Twelve and the Presidency of the Seventy, anointing their heads with consecrated oil and receiving blessings. At the close of the meeting, the gift of tongues was manifested, and angels mingled their voices with those present; praises swelled in the bosoms of all present for the space of half an hour.[8] This anointing was given in preparation for the endowment that would be given in the Kirtland Temple, following its dedication.

Though it is not recorded by the Prophet, Elder Heber C. Kimball has stated that when the Twelve were anointed "John [who was a member of the ancient First Presidency] stood in their midst," while Peter [the senior Apostle] was "in the stand."[9] In one sermon, Elder Kimball said "that when Peter came and sat in the Temple in Kirtland, he had on a neat woolen garment, nicely adjusted around the neck."[10] Later, Elder Kimball declared that he could "bring twenty witnesses" who beheld these ancient personages.[11]

PROPHETS, SEERS, AND REVELATORS

On Sunday, March 27, 1836, the doors of the newly completed Kirtland Temple opened for the dedicatory services. This was the first temple to be dedicated in this dispensation. It was built at great cost and sacrifice; however, the Saints counted it a great blessing to build a house to the Lord. After the congregation and the leading councils were seated, and after President Sidney Rigdon had spoken for two and a half hours to all present, he called upon the several quorums, commencing with the First Presidency, to manifest by standing their willingness to accept Joseph Smith as a prophet and seer, and to uphold him by their prayers of faith. All the quorums and then the congregation, each in turn, unanimously complied.

Following a twenty-minute recess, the Prophet made a short speech and called upon the quorums and the congregation to acknowledge all of the members of the Presidency as prophets and seers, and uphold them by their prayers. All stood.

Once again, the Prophet Joseph called upon the quorums and the congregation of Saints to acknowledge the Twelve Apostles, who were all present, as prophets, seers, and revelators, and special witnesses to all the nations of the earth, holding the keys of the kingdom. The quorums and the congregation each in turn stood.[12]

The prayer of dedication was then given by the Prophet Joseph, who received it by revelation (see D&C 109). Summarizing what happened in the Kirtland Temple, Elder Joseph Fielding Smith says, "At the dedication there were given to the saints some wonderful manifestations. The house was filled with heavenly beings, who were seen only by part of the congregation. Some had the privilege of a vision of the Savior. The spirit of prophecy rested upon a number of the leading brethren, and it was a feast of Pentecost to all who were assembled there."[13]

ORDINANCE OF WASHING OF FEET

At the last supper in Jerusalem, the Savior performed the gospel ordinance of washing of feet for the Twelve Apostles. He girded himself with a towel around his waist, poured water in a basin, and washed and wiped the feet of the Jewish Twelve (see John 13:1–17). Following this ordinance, the Lord said, "Ye call me Master and Lord: and ye say well; for so I am. If I then, your Lord and Master, have washed your feet; ye also ought to wash one another's feet. For I have given you an example, that ye should do as I have done to you" (see John 13:13–15).

As part of the restoration of all things in this the dispensation of the fulness of times, the sacred ordinance of washing of feet was restored through the Prophet Joseph Smith. In a revelation given December 27, 1832, the Lord gave the following command, "Sanctify yourselves; yea, purify your hearts, and cleanse your hands and your feet before me, that I may make you clean; That I may testify unto your Father, and your God, and my God, that you are clean from the blood of this wicked generation" (D&C 88:74–75).

In this same revelation, the Lord commanded that the School of the Prophets be established. Rules of conduct were given for those who attended this house of learning. This school was to be established for the benefit and learning of all who were "called to the ministry in the church" (D&C 88:127; see also 88:128–137). The Lord then declared, "And ye shall not receive any among you into this school save he is clean from the blood of this generation; And he shall be received by the ordinance of the washing of feet, for unto this end was the ordinance of the washing of feet instituted" (D&C 88:138–139). This ordinance is to be administered by the president of the Church; it is to begin by prayer; and after partaking of the emblems of the sacrament, the president "is to gird himself according to the pattern given in the thirteenth chapter of John's testimony concerning me" (D&C 88:141; see also John 13:1–17).

In compliance with this revelation, the Prophet Joseph on January

23, 1833, girded a towel around his waist and washed and wiped the feet of the members of the School of the Prophets. Speaking of this ordinance, the Prophet says: "By the power of the Holy Ghost I pronounced them all clean from the blood of this generation."[14]

After the Twelve Apostles were chosen and ordained, Joseph Smith attended a council meeting of the Twelve on Monday, October 5, 1835, and gave them instruction concerning their duties. He further instructed them to attend to the ordinance of the washing of feet.[15]

Then, on Thursday, November 12, 1835, the Prophet met with the Twelve again. During his remarks to them, he said:

> The item to which I wish the more particularly to call your attention to-night, is the ordinance of washing of feet. This we have not done as yet, but it is necessary now, as much as it was in the days of the Savior; and we must have a place prepared, that we may attend to this ordinance aside from the world. . . .
>
> The house of the Lord must be prepared, and the solemn assembly called and organized in it, according to the order of the house of God; and in it we must attend to the ordinance of washing of feet. It was never intended for any but official members [of the Church]. It is calculated to unite our hearts, that we may be one in feeling and sentiment, and that our faith may be strong, so that Satan cannot overthrow us, nor have any power over us here [on earth].
>
> The endowment you are so anxious about, you cannot comprehend now . . . [but] when we meet in the solemn assembly . . . [when] all the official members shall meet, we must be clean every whit.[16]

Following the temple dedication on Wednesday, March 30, 1836, tubs, water, and towels were prepared in this sacred house of the Lord. The First Presidency, the Twelve, the Seventies, and all the official members of the Church, amounting to about three hundred, participated in the ordinance of washing of feet as previously described. As it pertains to the Apostles, the members of the First Presidency washed the feet of the Twelve, pronouncing many prophecies and blessings upon them. Afterwards, the Twelve washed the feet of the Presidents of the several quorums.[17]

REASONS FOR THE ORDINANCE

For the same reasons that the Lord performed the ordinance of washing of feet for the Jewish Twelve, the First Presidency, under the direction of President Joseph Smith, performed this ordinance for the Twelve Apostles on March 30, 1836. Those reasons include the following:

- So that the Lord can pronounce these special witnesses clean from the blood of this wicked generation (see D&C 88:74–75, 138).
- To unite their hearts, so that they may be one in feeling and sentiment, and that their faith may be strong, so that Satan cannot overthrow them, nor have any power over them on this earth (see DHC, Vol. 2, 309).

"ONLY A PARTIAL ENDOWMENT"

Elder McConkie writes:

> It should be remembered that the endowment given [of washing of feet, and receiving spiritual blessings] in the Kirtland Temple was only a partial endowment, and that the full endowment was not performed until the saints had established themselves in Nauvoo. (*Doctrines of Salvation*, vol. 2, pp. 241–242) The full endowment—referred to in the revelation dated January 19, 1841 (D&C 124:36–41)—including washings and anointings, except under unusual circumstances, is designated to be administered in the temples of the Lord.
>
> Thus the knowledge relative to the washing of feet has been revealed step by step in this day until a full knowledge is now incorporated in the revealed ordinances of the Lord's house.[18]

Concerning this "partial endowment" in the Kirtland Temple, Elder Joseph Fielding Smith explains that it "is of double meaning. First, there were to come from on high essential blessings for the saints, which up to that time had not been revealed. Second, the elders were to receive greater powers that they might be better qualified to teach. It was made known by many manifestations of divine power at the dedication that the temple had been accepted as the house of the Lord."[19]

From this statement, we learn that in addition to other elders of the Church, the members of the Quorum of the Twelve, as Saints, would also receive essential ordinances and blessings in the Kirtland Temple. Following the ordinance of washing of feet and receiving blessings from the First Presidency, the Twelve were better qualified to teach the gospel of Jesus Christ.[20]

CHAPTER 6

THE FAITHFUL SIX

As explained previously, the Twelve Apostles who were chosen and ordained by the Three Witnesses were later organized according to age. On May 2, 1835, the Prophet Joseph said it would be the duty of the Twelve, when in council, to take their seats together according to age, the oldest to be seated at the head.[1] In a footnote, Elder B. H. Roberts adds, "It should be observed here, that this arrangement has reference only to the first organization of the quorum of the Twelve. After this first arrangement, the brethren of that quorum held and now hold their place in it and preside according to seniority of ordination, not of age."[2]

Based on the remarks given by the Prophet on May 2, 1835, Elder Thomas B. Marsh became the President of the Twelve.[3]

What became of Elder Marsh and others of the first Apostles called and chosen in this dispensation? To answer, we turn to the words of President Joseph F. Smith of the First Presidency:

> It is astonishing to think of the great number from the beginning [of the organization of the Church in 1830] to the present, who have embraced the Gospel and then have fallen away. Even of the first Twelve Apostles who have been ordained to that high and holy calling nearly one-half had apostatized from the faith within two or three years of their ordination. The trials and temptations to which they were exposed were more than they were able to endure, and therefore they fell by the way and turned from the truth. So with many of the

members of the Church who embraced the faith, and were then overcome by the allurements of the world and the influence of the Evil one.[4]

With this understanding, we will provide a brief description of the ministry of each of the original Twelve Apostles. Concerning the oldest member, President Thomas B. Marsh, Elder George A. Smith relates the following story:

> While the Saints were living in Far West, there were two sisters wishing to make cheese, and, neither of them possessing the requisite number of cows, they agreed to exchange milk. The wife of Thomas B. Marsh, who was then the President of the Twelve Apostles, and Sister Harris concluded they would exchange milk, in order to make a little larger cheese than they otherwise could. To be sure to have justice done, it was agreed that they should not save the strippings [to finish a milking by pressing out the last available milk], but that the milk and strippings should all go together.[5]

Mrs. Harris performed her part of the agreement, but Mrs. Marsh kept a pint of "strippings" from each cow. When this became known, it was brought before the teachers, who decided against Mrs. Marsh. An appeal was taken to the bishop, and he sustained the decision of the teachers. President Marsh should have righted the wrong, but instead he sided with his wife and appealed to the high council. The council upheld the bishop's decision. President Marsh then appealed to the First Presidency, and Joseph and his two counselors agreed to review the case. They approved the decision of the high council. Not satisfied with that decision, Marsh declared that "he would sustain the character of his wife, even if he had to go to hell for it."

Elder George A. Smith concluded by saying:

> The then President of the Twelve Apostles, the man who should have been the first to do justice and cause reparation to be made for wrong, committed by any member of his family, took that position, and what next? He went before a magistrate and swore that the 'Mormons' were hostile towards the State of Missouri. That

affidavit brought from the government of Missouri an extermination order, which drove some 15,000 Saints from their homes and habitations, and some thousands perished through suffering the exposure consequent on this state of affairs.[6]

For his actions, Thomas B. Marsh was excommunicated from the Church on March 17, 1839.[7] He returned to the Church and was rebaptized on July 16, 1857.[8]

Elder David W. Patten was the second oldest member of the Twelve. His ministry as a missionary and as an Apostle was highlighted by miracles, healings, and acts of faith. He twice saw Cain, who killed his brother Abel.[9] After having expressed his desire to be a martyr for the Church, he was killed October 25, 1838, at the battle of Crooked River, Missouri, at age thirty-eight. The Prophet Joseph wrote, "Brother David Patten was a very worthy man, beloved by all good men who knew him. He was one of the Twelve Apostles, and died as he had lived, a man of God, and strong in the faith of a glorious resurrection, in a world where mobs will have no power or place. One of his last expressions to his wife was—'Whatever you do else, O! do not deny the faith.'"[10]

Elder Brigham Young was the third oldest member of the Twelve. He loved and revered the Prophet Joseph Smith.[11] On one occasion, he expressed these feelings, "I feel like shouting hallelujah, all the time, when I think that I ever knew Joseph Smith, the Prophet."[12]

It is important to note that Brigham Young was the second Apostle ordained into the Quorum of the Twelve by the Three Witnesses on February 14, 1835; Lyman E. Johnson was the first. After Lyman E. Johnson was excommunicated on April 13, 1838, Brigham Young became president of the Twelve by virtue of his seniority of ordination and his age.[13]

Following the martyrdom of the Prophet Joseph, Brother Brigham was sustained as the second president of the Church on December 27, 1847, at age forty-six.[14] He is regarded as one of the greatest colonizers in American history. Much has been written of this remarkable man. This, however, is what Elder George Q. Cannon said of him, "On my part, he [Brigham Young] was in my eyes as perfect a man as I ever knew. I never desired to see his faults: I closed my eyes to them. To me he was a prophet of God, the head of the dispensation on the earth, holding the keys under the Prophet Joseph, and in my mind there clustered about him, holding this position, everything holy and sacred and revered."[15]

Elder Heber C. Kimball was the fourth oldest member of the Twelve. He was blessed both by the First Presidency and the Spirit of the Lord with the "gift of winning souls." As a missionary to England, and in his Apostolic ministry, he was instrumental in bringing "salvation to thousands."[16] At different times in his ministry as an Apostle, his statements were prophetic. He was a gifted speaker and taught many truths of the gospel. He served faithfully in his Apostolic calling and was sustained as first counselor to President Brigham Young on December 27, 1847, at age forty-six.[17] Elder Joseph Fielding Smith wrote about him, saying, "He was one of the original members called into the council of the Twelve, and the 'father' of the British Mission. President Kimball was greatly blessed with the spirit of prophecy; was bold and fearless, and never faltered in his integrity to the truth."[18]

Elder Orson Hyde was the fifth oldest member of the Twelve. He served a mission to several states and served satisfactorily as an Apostle until he endorsed an inflammatory affidavit written and signed by President Thomas B. Marsh.[19] For his actions, Elder Hyde lost his Apostleship. He returned repentant to the body of the Church in June 1839, and with tears of humility begged forgiveness from the Brethren for his part in the report with Thomas B. Marsh. At a Conference of the Twelve held in Commerce (Nauvoo), Illinois, on June 27, 1839, Brother Hyde made his confession and was reinstated in the Quorum of the Twelve.[20] He served with Elder Heber C. Kimball on a mission in the British Isles.[21] Most significantly, he dedicated Palestine for the gathering of the Jews.[22]

Elder William E. McLellin was the sixth oldest member of the Twelve. When he first joined the Church, the revelations and commandments given through the Prophet were being prepared for publication. At a conference to consider their publication, he was one who questioned the language of the revelations and commandments. The Prophet received a revelation from the Lord directing him to invite the "most wise among you" to chose one of the least revelations and attempt to make one like unto it. If this proved to be a failure, then they would be "under condemnation" if they did not bear record that the revelations are true (see D&C 67). William E. McLellin, "as the wisest man," accepted the challenge from the Lord. His attempt was a failure, to the convincing of the elders present. These same elders signified their willingness to bear testimony to the world of the truth of the revelations given to the Prophet Joseph.[23]

Following this experience, he served faithfully for a time. Then, on May 11, 1838, a Church trial was held, wherein Brother McLellin stated that he had no confidence in the leaders of the Church, believing they had transgressed. Consequently he had quit praying, did not keep the commandments, and had indulged in his lustful desires.[24] In addition to this statement, other sources confirm that William E. McLellin was excommunicated from the Church at Far West on this same day.[25]

Elder Parley P. Pratt [the brother to Orson] was the seventh oldest member of the Twelve. He was faithful until the summer of 1837, when he began to openly express that the Prophet Joseph was in error. Brother Pratt made things right with the Prophet and was restored to full fellowship.[26] Thereafter, he served faithfully until he was assassinated on May 13, 1857, near Van Buren, Arkansas, at age fifty. Elder Joseph Fielding Smith wrote of Elder Pratt, saying, "One of the greatest expounders of the latter-day faith, a poet and writer, whose works survive and have done much to bring many to a knowledge of the Gospel."[27]

Elder Luke S. Johnson [the brother to Lyman] was the eighth oldest member of the Twelve. In 1837, the spirit of apostasy developed with certain members in the leading councils of the Church. Some began to be critical of the Prophet and the Church. One of these was Luke S. Johnson. On December 10, 1837, Presidents Joseph Smith and Sidney Rigdon returned from Missouri to Kirtland, Ohio. During their absence, certain members of the leading councils had decided to overthrow the Church, and Luke S. Johnson was involved.[28] Because of his apostasy, he was excommunicated on April 13, 1838.[29] He returned to the Church and was baptized again in 1846 in Nauvoo.[30] Brother Johnson came West with the original pioneers in 1847. In 1858, he settled St. John, Tooele County, Utah, and when the ward was organized there, he became the bishop. "He died in the house of his brother-in-law, Orson Hyde, in Salt Lake City" in 1861.[31]

Elder William Smith (who is the Prophet's brother) was the ninth oldest member of the Twelve. Because of his "excitable disposition," he was very verbal at times with his presiding brothers, Joseph and Hyrum.[32] On one occasion, he became so enraged that he physically assaulted the Prophet and others.[33] After the martyrdom of the Prophet, Brother Smith was excommunicated on October 12, 1845.[34] On October 19, 1845, it is written, "William Smith who has published a pamphlet against the Twelve was excommunicated from the church by unanimous vote."[35]

Elder Orson Pratt [the brother of Parley], age twenty-three, was the tenth oldest member of the Twelve. In 1842, he became lukewarm toward the work and was excommunicated from the Church on August 20, 1842, for disobedience.[36] In January 1843, the confidence of the Prophet was restored to Elder Pratt.[37] On January 20, 1843, the Prophet attended a council meeting of the Twelve. During this meeting, he said the council had been called to consider the case of Orson Pratt, who was present. Later that afternoon, Orson Pratt and his wife were baptized in the Mississippi River; they were then confirmed members of the Church. The Prophet ordained Elder Pratt to his former office in the Quorum of the Twelve.[38] Thereafter, he served faithfully.

"I do not know of a man who is more willing to do what he is told than he is," said President Young about Elder Pratt. "If he is told to teach mathematics, he is willing to do it; if he is told to make books, preach the Gospel, work in a garden or tend cattle, he is willing to do it, and I know of no man more willing to do anything and everything required of him than he is."[39] President Young further said, "If Elder Pratt was chopped up in inch pieces, each piece would cry out Mormonism is true!"[40]

President Heber J. Grant echoed these sentiments, saying Orson Pratt "was one of the greatest writers and defenders of the truth the Church has ever had."[41]

Elder John F. Boynton was the eleventh oldest member of the Twelve. Because of his involvement with apostasy in 1837,[42] he was excommunicated on January 1, 1838.[43]

Elder Lyman E. Johnson [brother to Luke] was the twelfth oldest member of the Twelve. As was mentioned previously, he was the first Apostle ordained by the Three Witnesses on February 14, 1835.[44] Due to his apostate actions in 1837,[45] he was excommunicated on April 13, 1838.[46]

While it is true that Elders Orson Hyde and Orson Pratt were temporarily dropped from the Quorum of the Twelve Apostles, after they were reinstated in the Twelve, they remained faithful until their deaths. Concerning the original Twelve Apostles, the following six were faithful to the Apostolic calling: Elders David W. Patten, Brigham Young, Heber C. Kimball, Orson Hyde, Parley P. Pratt, and Orson Pratt.

Regarding those who apostatized, Elder Ezra Taft Benson made the observation that "six of the original Twelve Apostles selected by [the Three Witnesses, under the direction of] Joseph Smith were excommunicated. The Three Witnesses [Oliver Cowdery, David Whitmer, and Martin Harris] to the *Book of Mormon* left the Church. Three of Joseph's counselor's [Sidney Rigdon, Frederick G. Williams, William Law] fell—one [Law] even helped plot his death."[47]

"A natural question that might arise would be, that if the Lord knew in advance that these men would fall, as he undoubtedly did, why did he have his Prophet call them to such high office? The answer is: to fill the Lord's purposes."[48]

Agency is one of the greatest gifts that our Heavenly Father gives to each of us. Therefore, it must not be believed that because of the Lord's foreknowledge of what would happen under given conditions with these six Apostles that it was a determining cause of their downfall. He never took away their agency. They chose their actions, even though these leaders were a cause of sorrow and embarrassment to the Prophet and the Lord's Church.

OTHERS CALLED TO THE APOSTLESHIP

Due to the apostasy and excommunication of six of the original Twelve Apostles, others were called to fill their vacancy. In a response to the Prophet's supplication concerning the Twelve, a revelation from the Lord was given on July 8, 1838, counseling the Prophet to fill the places of those who had fallen. The Lord also gave the names of four Brethren who were to be called (see D&C 118:6).[49]

In addition to the four men named in this revelation, the Prophet received inspiration to call three others. They are listed in the order of their calling and ordination as Apostles:

Elder John E. Page, at age thirty-nine, was ordained on December 19, 1838, under the hands of President Brigham Young, then president of the Twelve, and Elder Heber C. Kimball, at Far West.[50] When he was set apart to accompany Elder Orson Hyde on a mission to Palestine, he failed to make the journey.[51] For his rebellious attitude, his fellow members of the Twelve wrote, "We . . . have no fellowship with Elder John E. Page, in consequence of his murmuring disposition, and choosing to absent himself from our councils, and then saying that he is made a servant and slave of by his quorum. . . . He has been on the background and in the shade ever since he failed to fulfill his mission to Jerusalem in company with Elder Hyde."[52] John E. Page was excommunicated on June 27, 1846.[53]

Elder John Taylor, at age thirty, was ordained on December 19, 1838, under the hands of President Brigham Young and Elder Heber

C. Kimball.⁵⁴ During those trying times when many were apostatizing from the Church, and from the Quorum of the Twelve, Elder Taylor stood nobly by the Prophet Joseph Smith.

While with the Prophet in Carthage Jail, Elder Taylor sang his favorite hymn, "A Poor Wayfaring Man of Grief." When the mob began firing shots, the Prophet and his brother Hyrum were killed. Elder Taylor was severely wounded with four wounds but recovered, and another member at the jail, Willard Richards received only a minor wound to his ear.⁵⁵ One of Elder Taylor's best writings is his record of the martyrdom of Joseph and Hyrum (see D&C 135).⁵⁶ Elder Taylor was a gifted singer, writer, and speaker. "He filled numerous missions and opened the door for the preaching of the gospel in France in 1850. He superintended the translation of the Book of Mormon in French and German, and was engaged in literary work at home and abroad covering a period of many years."⁵⁷ He was sustained as president of the Church on October 10, 1880, at age seventy-one.⁵⁸

Elder Wilford Woodruff, at age thirty-two, was ordained on April 26, 1839, by President Brigham Young.⁵⁹ Elder Woodruff was a loyal and faithful Apostle. He was a gifted missionary who brought many into the Church both in England and the United States. He was sustained as president of the Church on April 7, 1889, at age eighty-two.⁶⁰ "If I were to describe President Woodruff in one word that would best describe him, I would choose the word *spirituality,*" wrote Elder Boyd K. Packer. "A man of deep spiritual attunement, from the days of his youth he had received and responded to spiritual guidance; and it was this trait, perhaps above any other, that qualified him for a call to be a member of the Quorum of the Twelve Apostles."⁶¹ By command of the Lord, President Woodruff issued the Manifesto suspending the practice of plural marriage.⁶² He dedicated the Salt Lake Temple on April 6, 1893.⁶³ "He served for many years as Church historian, and kept remarkable journals, recording in detail all important events of which he was a witness."⁶⁴

Elder George A. Smith, at age twenty-one, was ordained on April 26, 1839, by Elder Heber C. Kimball.⁶⁵ He was a cousin of Joseph and Hyrum Smith, and he served faithfully as a missionary to England, accompanying Elder Heber C. Kimball. During those trying times when many were apostatizing from the Church and the Quorum of the Twelve, Elder Smith remained faithful. When the Saints were forced to leave Nauvoo, Elder Smith, along with President Brigham Young and Willard Richards, crossed the Mississippi for their long trek to the west. On the first Sabbath in the Salt Lake Valley, he preached a sermon with Elders Heber C. Kimball, Ezra T. Benson, and Willard Richards. After the death of President Willard Richards, second counselor to President Young, Elder Smith was called to be the Church historian; he was sustained as first counselor to President Brigham Young on October 6, 1868, at age fifty-one.[66]

Elder Willard Richards, at age thirty-five, was ordained on April 14, 1840, by President Brigham Young.[67] He served faithfully in his Apostolic calling. When President Heber C. Kimball died, he was sustained as second counselor to President Brigham Young on December 27, 1847, at age forty-three.[68]

Elder Lyman Wight, at age forty-four, was ordained by President Joseph Smith at Nauvoo, Illinois, on April 8, 1841.[69] Concerning this call, President Joseph Smith said that it was necessary to fill the vacancy of the late David W. Patten. President Rigdon nominated Elder Lyman Wight to that office, and he was unanimously accepted.[70] Nearly eight years later, he was excommunicated on February 12, 1849.[71]

Elder Amasa M. Lyman, at twenty-nine, was ordained by President Brigham Young and Elders Heber C. Kimball and George A. Smith on August 20, 1842, to replace William Smith.[72] It is worth noting that he was replaced in the Quorum of the Twelve Apostles on January 20, 1843, due to reinstatement of Elder Orson Pratt.[73] He was then appointed a counselor in the First Presidency in February 1843, was returned to the Quorum of the Twelve on August 12, 1844,[74] and then, due to apostasy, was excommunicated on May 12, 1870. Concerning his calling, Elder Lyman made this remark: "Says one, 'Were you always an Apostle?' No. 'Were you ordained an Apostle?' Yes. 'What did that do for you?' It only connected me with twelve men; it did not give me any more knowledge, or make me any different."[75] His blessings were restored after his death.[76]

From this information, we are informed of the first Apostolic succession of the Church in this final dispensation. Each was relatively young when called by the Lord, through His chosen servants; each had agency to fulfill their calling; and each chose to remain faithful or not.

CHAPTER 7

THE TWELVE LEAD THE CHURCH

AUTHORITY AND KEYS OF THE TWELVE

As was explained previously, the Melchizedek Priesthood and all the keys of all dispensations were bestowed upon Joseph Smith and Oliver Cowdery.[1] Though he was not an ordained member of the Quorum of the Twelve Apostles, the Prophet Joseph was the first Apostle in this dispensation.[2] On January 25 and 26, 1832, he was ordained and sustained as the president of the High Priesthood of the Church.[3] Then, on March 18, 1833, the First Presidency of the Church was first organized, with Joseph Smith as president and Sidney Rigdon and Frederick G. Williams as first and second counselors.[4] Therefore, Brother Joseph was the acknowledged and revered prophet and president of The Church of Jesus Christ of Latter-day Saints.

Our attention now turns to a council meeting of the newly called Twelve Apostles held on March 28, 1835, in Kirtland, Ohio. Each member was confessing their individual weaknesses and shortcomings, expressing repentance, and seeking a revelation of the Lord through his Prophet and Seer, for their mission assignment, which was to begin on May 4, 1835.[5] In a most humble petition, the Prophet says, "I inquired of the Lord, and received for answer the following revelation," then follows the revelation as recorded in Doctrine and Covenants section 107.[6] In this *revelation on the priesthood,* the Lord reveals this doctrine, "Of the Melchizedek Priesthood, three Presiding High Priests, chosen by the body, appointed and ordained to that office, and upheld by the confidence, faith, and prayer of the church, form a quorum of the Presidency of the Church" (D&C 107:22).

The Lord then states, "The twelve traveling councilors are called to be the Twelve Apostles, or special witnesses of the name of Christ in all the world. . . . And they form a quorum, equal in authority and power to the three presidents previously mentioned" (vv. 23–24).

Also, "The Seventy are also called to preach the gospel, and to be especial witnesses unto the Gentiles and in all the world. . . . And they form a quorum, equal in authority to that of the Twelve special witnesses or Apostles just named" (vv. 25–26).

Therefore, from this revealed doctrine, we learn that where there is no First Presidency, the Quorum of the Twelve Apostles have the authority to preside. This is a critical doctrine of the Church! This is supported by what the Prophet said, "The Twelve are not subject to any other than the First Presidency, viz., myself, Sidney Rigdon, and Frederick G. Williams, who are now my Counselors; and where I am not, there is no First Presidency over the Twelve."[7] Providing additional information, Elder Joseph Fielding Smith says:

> The twelve are equal in authority and power to the three members of The First Presidency. The fact that it is also stated that the Seventies hold equal authority, has caused some misunderstanding. It is impossible, of course, for two, much less three councils, to have equal authority and power at the same time. If that were the case, there could be no head. The interpretation of these statements is that the Twelve Apostles hold all the authority and power that is vested in the First Presidency. But, it cannot be exercised as long as the First Presidency is intact. On the death of the President of the Church, the First Presidency is dissolved, and then the Council of the Twelve Apostles exercises all the authority that was vested in the First Presidency, and this continues until the First Presidency is organized again and becomes the presiding council in the Church. If the time should ever come, which is improbable, when both the First Presidency and the entire Quorum of the Twelve Apostles should be destroyed, then, and only then, would The First Council of the Seventy [meaning: The First Quorum of the Seventy] have the power and the authority mentioned in the revelation. In no other way are these three councils equal

in authority, and the First Presidency holds the keys of authority while the President of the Church is living.[8]

In addition to the revelation on the priesthood, President Wilford Woodruff, as president the Church, publicly declared the following:

> I bear my testimony that in the early spring of 1844 in Nauvoo, the Prophet Joseph Smith called the Twelve Apostles together, and he delivered unto them the ordinances of the Church and kingdom of God; and all the keys and powers that God had bestowed upon him, he sealed upon our heads. He told us we must round up our shoulders and bear off this kingdom or we would be damned. I am the only man now living in the flesh who heard that testimony from his mouth, and I know this is true by the power of God manifest through him.
>
> At that meeting he stood on his feet about three hours and taught us the things of the kingdom. His face was as clear as amber, and he was covered with power that I have never seen in any man in the flesh before.[9]

In August of that same year, President Woodruff provided this additional information:

> He [the Prophet] said, 'Brethren, the Lord Almighty has sealed upon my head every Priesthood, every key, every power, every principle that belongs to the last dispensation of the fulness of times, and to the building up of the kingdom of God. [Concerning the Twelve, the Prophet said:] I have sealed upon your heads all those principles, Priesthood, Apostleship, and keys of the kingdom of God and now you have got to round up your shoulders and bear off this kingdom or you will be damned.' I do not forget those words—I never shall while I live. That was the last speech he ever made in the flesh. Soon afterwards he was martyred and called home to glory.[10]

Last, Elder Orson Hyde of the Twelve, said: "'Before I went east on the 4th of April [1844] last, we were in council with Brother Joseph almost every day for weeks; said Brother Joseph in one of those councils, 'There is something going to happen; I don't know what it is, but the Lord bids me to hasten and give you your endowment before the [Nauvoo] Temple is finished.' He conducted us through every ordinance of the holy priesthood, and when he had gone through with all the ordinances he rejoiced very much, and said, 'Now if they kill me, you have got all the keys, and all the ordinances, and you can confer them upon others, and the hosts of Satan will not be able to tear down the kingdom as fast [as] you will be able to built it up'; and now, said he, 'On your shoulders will the responsibility of leading this people to rest.'"[11]

Thus, the Prophet, sensing his impending death, conferred upon the Twelve Apostles all of the keys and authority he held. It is worth emphasizing that he did not confer the keys and authority on one member only but upon each member individually and upon the Quorum collectively.

Transfiguration of Brigham Young

The martyrdom of President Joseph Smith and his brother Hyrum, the patriarch and assistant president of the Church,[12] at Carthage Jail on June 27, 1844,[13] "came as a terrible shock to the members of the Church. The thought that the Prophet was to be taken from them had not entered their minds, notwithstanding the many predictions he had made regarding his approaching death."[14]

The death of the Prophet brought about the first disorganization of the presiding priesthood quorum—the First Presidency. Though the revelation on priesthood had been given in 1835 (see D&C 107), there had been no consideration or established procedure on how the Twelve were to function following the death of a president of the Church.

Not following the will of the Lord to stay in Nauvoo, Sidney Rigdon, first counselor to President Smith, moved his family from Nauvoo, Illinois, to Pittsburgh, Pennsylvania (see D&C 124:108–9). This and various other actions manifested a spirit of apostasy. When word of Joseph's and Hyrum's martyrdom reached Sidney Rigdon, he traveled sixteen hundred miles to Nauvoo, where he arrived on Saturday, August 3, 1844.

Most of the Apostles were in the Eastern States serving missions when the Prophet and his brother were martyred. This is what President Brigham Young thought after hearing of the martyrdom:

> When I first heard of Joseph's death the first flash across my mind was 'are the keys of the priesthood here?' I sat leaning in a chair, with Orson Pratt upon my left, and

I had no more idea of it falling upon me than of the most unlikely thing in the world, and I felt it come like a flash of lightening to my mind, and I said, 'the keys of the kingdom are here.' I did not think it was with me, [because it was not necessary to exercise those keys of Presidency while the Prophet was alive] but I felt that they were here, but knew that it was the Lord's business.[15]

Elders Parley P. Pratt and George A. Smith had arrived in Nauvoo a few days before Sidney Rigdon did. The Apostles invited Sidney Rigdon to meet with them on Sunday morning at the home of the wounded Elder John Taylor. Instead of meeting with the Apostles as he had agreed, Sidney met with William Marks and others and made plans for the appointment of a trustee-in-trust and a "guardian" for the Church, before others of the Twelve could arrive back in Nauvoo. A public meeting was held at ten o' clock, and Sidney Rigdon preached to the Saints stating that a "guardian" must be appointed "to build up the Church unto Joseph," and stating that he, Sidney, was the man spoken of by the ancient prophets to do the work they had spoken of by prophecy. Another meeting was held in the afternoon, where William Marks, president of the Nauvoo Stake, announced that there would be a special meeting on Thursday, August 8, "for the purpose of choosing a guardian." Sidney had requested that the meeting be held on August 6, but President Marks announced it for two days later, which proved providential, for President Brigham Young and most of the other Apostles arrived in Nauvoo on the evening of the sixth.

On Wednesday, August 7, 1844, Sidney Rigdon met with most of the Twelve Apostles, the high council, and the high priests at the Seventies Hall. At this meeting, President Rigdon related a vision he said he'd had, and stated that there could be no successor to Joseph Smith, but that the Church must be built up to him. Sidney further said that he was a spokesman for Joseph, and he proposed to be a guardian to the Church, if the Saints would have him.

President Brigham Young then spoke and said that he did not care who leads the Church, "but one thing I must know, and that is what God says about it." Continuing, he said, "Joseph conferred upon our heads all the keys and powers belonging to the Apostleship which he himself held before he was taken away, and no man or set of men can get between Joseph and the Twelve in this world or in the world to come.

"How often has Joseph said to the Twelve, 'I have laid the foundation and you must build thereon, for upon your shoulders the kingdom rests.'"[16]

This statement reaffirms what President Wilford Woodruff and Elder Orson Hyde had written, which we have recorded earlier in this chapter. Though the Prophet had given all the keys to the Twelve, a special meeting was held in the morning on Thursday, August 8, 1844, for the members of the Church in Nauvoo to hear Sidney Rigdon's proposal to be a "guardian" of the Church. After Sidney Rigdon spoke for an hour and a half, the Saints were more convinced that Brother Rigdon was without the inspiration of the Lord, and they left the meeting feeling he was not the man to lead them. In his private journal, William Hyde, who would become the first bishop in Hyde Park, Cache County, Utah, wrote:

> On Thursday, August the 8th, I attended a special conference in Nauvoo. . . . Elder Rigdon sought, as he expressed it, the guardianship of the Church, but it was plainly manifest that the Spirit of the Lord had withdrawn from him, and that he sought that which did not belong to him.

He then interjects this comment:

> From the time the saints were driven from Missouri he had evidently been on the background, and had not walked up to his station, and on one occasion I heard Joseph Smith say that he had carried Elder Rigdon on his back long enough, and then turning to the Twelve said that if they did not help him at that time in shaking him off, the time would come when they would have it to do, and that without his, Joseph's assistance. And on Thursday, the 8th of August, was this saying of the Prophet brought home with weight to my mind.

Returning to the meeting held in the afternoon, Brother Hyde continues:

> President Young . . . then called upon the saints to know if they would receive the Twelve and let them stand in their place as the First Presidency of the Church in the absence of Joseph. The vote was unanimous in the affirmative. *On this day it was plainly manifest that*

the mantle of Joseph had rested upon President Young. The voice of the same spirit by which he, Joseph, spake was this day sounded in our ears, so much so that I once, unthoughtedly, raised my head to see if it was not actually Joseph addressing the assembly.[17]

In addition to this statement, Elder Joseph Fielding Smith, the Church historian at the time, recorded this testimony:

> President Brigham Young addressed the congregation. He spoke with great power and the people were convinced that the authority and power of the presidency was with the Apostles. When he first arose to speak the people were greatly astonished, for President Young stood transfigured before them and they beheld the Prophet Joseph Smith and heard his voice as naturally as ever they did when he was living. [He then writes these declarative words:] It was a manifestation to the Saints that they might recognize the correct authority.[18]

Others in the congregation also heard the voice of the Prophet Joseph Smith, while still others beheld the Prophet and heard his voice. Through this transfiguration, the Lord instructed the Saints that the Twelve Apostles, with President Brigham Young at their head, were the presiding council of the Church.

Following President Young's address in the afternoon, Amasa M. Lyman, William W. Phelps, and Parley P. Pratt each spoke endorsing those remarks. Once again, President Young arose and spoke to the congregation. His original intent was to ask the Saints whether or not they wanted Sidney Rigdon to be a "guardian" for the Church; however, at the request of Brother Rigdon, he instead presented the question of supporting the Apostles as the presiding quorum of the Church. He said:

> Does the Church want, and is it their only desire to sustain the Twelve as the First Presidency of this people?
>
> Here are the Apostles, the Bible, the Book of Mormon, the Doctrine and Covenants—they are written on the tablet of my heart. If the Church want the Twelve to stand as the head, the First Presidency of

the Church, and at the head of this kingdom in all the world, stand next to Joseph, walk up into their calling, and hold the keys of this kingdom, every man, every woman, every quorum is now put in order, and you are now the sole controllers of it.[19]

The voting by raising the right hand was universal. President Young then called for any negative votes; no hands were raised. Following this, President Young noted this action superseded the question of presenting Sidney Rigdon as "guardian" and trying it by quorums.[20] Elder Joseph Fielding Smith observed:

> In this manner, the apostles, who were the rightful authorities according to the revelations of the Lord, were sustained by the vote of the people and by common consent, as the Lord had commanded that all things should be done. The matter of succession was properly and rightfully decided, and was now binding on the members of the Church. At the close of the services the Saints returned to their homes, their minds at rest, for they were, with very few exceptions, no longer in doubt regarding the authority of the Priesthood and the presidency of the Church.[21]

Concerning the authority and keys of the members of the Quorum of the Twelve Apostles, in 1861, President Brigham Young declared, "What ordination should a man receive to possess all the keys and powers of the Holy Priesthood. . . . He should be ordained an Apostle of Jesus Christ. That office puts him in possession of every key, every power, every authority, communication, benefit, blessing, glory, and kingdom that was ever revealed to man. That pertains to the office of an Apostle of Jesus Christ."[22]

From what is written in the great revelation on the priesthood (see D&C 107:21–24) and statements given by members of the Twelve, we know that the Twelve Apostles had the authority and keys to govern the Church following the martyrdom of Joseph and Hyrum Smith. In addition to that authority, they were upheld by the sustaining vote and confidence of the members of the Church. In harmony with this statement, President George Q. Cannon, of the First Presidency said:

> While the Prophet Joseph Smith lived no one supposed that any other man could be found who would have the power to lead the Church. The great bulk of the Church believed he would live till Jesus should come, and when he was martyred every heart was filled with sorrow. Who could take his place? Who could hold the keys? Who could lead the people? Confusion to a certain extent reigned in the midst of the people. But all the keys and authority which Joseph received from various angels, he conferred upon others before his death. These [twelve] men held the same authority, therefore, that the Prophet did; but because it was not necessary for them to exercise it, they did not appear to possess it. After Joseph was killed, and the occasion arose, then the man who held the keys, he being the senior apostle and the one who presided over the quorum of the Twelve, arose, filled with the same power, and with the same gifts—at least, with a great many of them. Men vary in their organizations. Joseph possessed gifts that no man in this age possesses. Brigham Young, having a different organization, had gifts which the Prophet did not have. . . .
>
> There was no First Presidency [after the death of the Prophet]. It fell then to the quorum of the Twelve to preside; for they held the authority equal to the First Presidency, and the First Presidency were absent. The quorum of the Twelve has no right to preside when the First Presidency is there. Brigham Young stepped forward with the Twelve and took the Presidency of the Church.[23]

Then President Cannon makes a most intriguing comment of President Young, saying, "And through his unwillingness to push himself forward, the Twelve governed the Church for three years."[24] To emphasize the importance of the presiding quorums in the Church, President Cannon notes:

> But the Church is not perfectly organized unless there is a First Presidency, and a Twelve, and a Seventy.

Now, every one of the Twelve held the same powers as the Prophet Joseph but they had not right to exercise them only in their own place and situation. No one of them could rise up and exercise the authority of leading the Church. As the Lord has plainly revealed, there is only one man on earth at a time who has the right to hold the keys and to preside [over the Church], though others may have equal power, authority and ordination, and be equal in every other respect. Only one man is called to lead. There were Twelve men with Brigham, but Brigham held the keys. He was the senior Apostle and had the right to exercise that authority. When the First Presidency was organized he still, with his counselors, had the right to preside over the Church.[25]

CHANGES IN THE TWELVE AND FIRST PRESIDENCY

Men who are called to the Quorum of the Twelve Apostles serve for life. The same applies to the president of the Church. President Spencer W. Kimball explained how changes are enacted when he said:

> Full provision has been made by our Lord for changes. Today there are fourteen apostles holding the keys in suspension, the twelve and the two counselors to the President, to be brought into use if and when circumstances allow, all ordained to leadership in their turn as they move forward in seniority.
>
> There have been some eighty apostles so endowed since [the Prophet] Joseph Smith, though only eleven have occupied the place of the President of the Church, death having intervened; and since the death of his servants is in the power and control of the Lord, he permits to come to the first place only the one who is destined to take that leadership. Death and life become the controlling factors. Each new apostle in turn is chosen by the Lord and revealed to the then living prophet who ordains him.[26]

Twenty days after he was ordained and set apart as the fifteenth president of the Church, President Gordon B. Hinckley spoke these words at the April 1, 1995, priesthood meeting:

> Concerning the First Presidency the Lord has said, "Of the Melchizedek Priesthood, three Presiding High Priests, chosen by the body, appointed and ordained to that office, and upheld by the confidence, faith, and prayer of the church" (D&C 107:22).
>
> I emphasize those words, "upheld by the confidence, faith, and prayer of the church."
>
> Your uplifted hands in the solemn assembly this morning became an expression of your willingness and desire to uphold us, your brethren and your servants, with your confidence, faith, and prayer. I am deeply grateful for that expression. I thank you, each of you. I assure you, as you already know, that in the processes of the Lord, there is no aspiring for office. As the Lord said to his disciples, "Ye have not chosen me, but I have chosen you, and ordained you" (John 15:16). This office is not one to be sought after. The right to select rests with the Lord. He is the master of life and death. His is the power to call. His is the power to take away. His is the power to retain. It is all in His hands.[27]

ORDAINED TO BE PRESIDENT OF THE CHURCH

As revealed through the Prophet Joseph Smith, each man who is ordained to the Apostleship receives all of the keys of the kingdom of God on earth. However, the full operation of those keys remains dormant in that man unless he becomes the senior Apostle. Only at that time, he is able to exercise the keys in their fulness. Elder Spencer W. Kimball said:

> When President [Heber J.] Grant died, and then when President [George Albert] Smith died, I, with my brethren, the Twelve Apostles, presided over all the Church by revelation. . . . Twice in my short spiritual life I have helped preside over the whole Church as one of the Twelve who had all of the keys. . . .

> The President who will be the President of the Church in 1975 has probably already been ordained and been given the keys by President [David O.] McKay, or it is quite likely by President Smith or by President Grant. The next President of the Church already holds the keys. He holds them in his pocket, dormant. But when the day comes when the Twelve preside, nominate, elect, and sustain him as President of the Church, the keys come out of his pocket, go into his hand, and they then begin to turn the locks in all of the gates from here to heaven and from here to exaltation. Only one man holds them actively at any one time, but every apostle—there are fifteen of us—every apostle has all of the keys from the day of his ordination as an Apostle, but they are dormant until and if and when he should become President of the Church. . . .
>
> The Lord knows right now who will be the next President of the Church, and the next after that, and the next after that, if time doesn't run out [before the Second Coming of the Lord]. The Lord knows now! He chooses an Apostle and then an Apostle as President of the Church. So the Lord chooses his future President, not the day that there is a vacancy in the Presidency, but years and years before. Isn't it glorious?[28]

When he became president of the Church, President Kimball said:

> I was ordained by [President] Heber J. Grant to be a high priest and later to be an apostle. And when I was made an apostle, I was made virtually the President of the Church. And that is true of all the Twelve Apostles. There are fifteen apostles. The President of the Church, his two counselors, and the Quorum of the Twelve. And every one of the apostles is ordained to become the President of the Church if circumstances are propitious [meaning: favorable]. No new authority is given to the man when he becomes the President; the keys of the kingdom that are put in his hands have been held dormant.[29]

President Harold B. Lee was ordained and set apart as the eleventh president of the Church on July 7, 1972, at age seventy-three. He unexpectedly passed away on December 26, 1973, at age seventy-four. His tenure as president of the Church was only one year and five months in length. President N. Eldon Tanner, who served as President Lee's first counselor, explained what happened after President Lee's passing:

> I would like to explain to you exactly what took place following the unexpected death of President Harold B. Lee on December 26, 1973. I was in Phoenix, Arizona, to spend Christmas with my daughter and her family when a call came to me from Arthur Haycock, secretary to President Lee. He said that President Lee was seriously ill, and he thought that I should plan to return home as soon as possible. A half-hour later he called and said: "The Lord has spoken. President Lee has been called home."
>
> President Romney [second counselor to President Lee], who in my absence was directing the affairs of the Church [as a member of the First Presidency] was at the hospital with President Spencer W. Kimball [who was the president] of the Council of the Twelve. Immediately upon President Lee's death President Romney turned to President Kimball and said, "You are in charge." Not one minute passed between the time President Lee died and the Twelve [Apostles] took over to preside over the Church.
>
> Following President Lee's funeral, President Kimball called a meeting of the Apostles for Sunday, December 30, at 3 p.m. in the Salt Lake Temple council room. President Romney and I had taken our respective places of seniority in the Council [of the Twelve Apostles], so there were fourteen of us present. Following a song, and prayer by President Romney, President Kimball, in deep humility, expressed his feelings to us. He said that he had spent Friday in the [Salt Lake] temple talking to the Lord, and he had shed many tears as he prayed for guidance in assuming his new responsibilities and in choosing his counselors.

Dressed in our temple robes, we held a prayer circle; President Kimball asked me [President Tanner] to conduct it and Elder Thomas S. Monson to offer the prayer. Following this, President Kimball explained the purpose of the meeting and called on each member of the Quorum in order of seniority, starting with Elder Ezra Taft Benson, to express his feelings as to whether the First Presidency should be organized that day or whether we should carry on as the Council of the Twelve. Each said, "We should organize now," and many complimentary things were spoken about President Kimball and his work with the Twelve.

Then Elder Ezra Taft Benson nominated Spencer W. Kimball to be the President of the Church. This was seconded by Elder Mark E. Petersen and unanimously approved. President Kimball then nominated his counselors: N. Eldon Tanner as first counselor, and Marion G. Romney as second, each of whom expressed a willingness to accept the position and devote his whole time and energy in serving in that capacity. They were unanimously approved. Then Elder Mark E. Petersen, second in seniority in the Twelve, nominated Ezra Taft Benson as President of the Quorum of the Twelve. This was unanimously approved.

At this point all the members present laid their hands upon the head of Spencer W. Kimball, and President Ezra Taft Benson was voice in blessing, ordaining, and setting apart Spencer W. Kimball as the Twelfth President of The Church of Jesus Christ of Latter-day Saints. Then, with President Kimball as voice, N. Eldon Tanner was set apart as first counselor and Marion G. Romney as second counselor in the First Presidency of the Church. Following the same procedure, he pronounced the blessing and setting apart of Ezra Taft Benson as President of the Quorum of the Twelve.[30]

Thus, the Lord determines changes made with members of the Twelve Apostles and the First Presidency. As has been stated, death and life become the controlling factors. The Son of God directs who will be the next Apostle or president of the Church. He alone determines who is called and how long that man will serve in the leading councils of His Church.

Therefore, it is important to emphasize that at the death of a president of the Church, the senior member of the Twelve Apostles—no matter who he is—has the authority, the keys, the right, and the obligation to lead and preside over the Church. This is who the Lord foreordained to be president of his Church at that time. Therefore, this revealed order of succession is a very important doctrine in the Church (see D&C 107:21–24).

CHAPTER 8

THE TWELVE AS THE FIRST PRESIDENCY

PRESIDENT BRIGHAM YOUNG

As mentioned earlier, a special meeting was held on August 8, 1844, for the members of the Church in Nauvoo to hear Sidney Rigdon's proposal to be a "guardian" of the Church. During this gathering, President Brigham Young, as president of the Twelve, said to the congregation, "Does the Church want, and is it their only desire to sustain the Twelve as the First Presidency of this people?" The voting was unanimous.[1] Elder Joseph Fielding Smith wrote about this special meeting, saying, "The matter of succession was properly and rightfully decided, and was now binding on the members of the Church."[2]

BRIGHAM YOUNG

It is interesting to note that after the Twelve Apostles were sustained as the First Presidency of the Church, each was given a designated name-title. The following is given by way of introduction:

> About the year 1844, Elder W. W. Phelps, wrote as follows, concerning the Twelve, in a paper called the *New York Prophet:*
>
> I know the Twelve, and they know me. Their names are: Brigham Young, the Lion of the Lord; Heber C. Kimball, the Herald of Grace; Parley P. Pratt, the Archer of Paradise; Orson Hyde, the Olive Branch of Israel;

Willard Richards, the Keeper of the Rolls; John Taylor, the Champion of Right; William Smith, the Patriarchal Staff of Jacob; Wilford Woodruff, the Banner of the Gospel; George A. Smith, the Entablature of Truth; Orson Pratt, the Guage of Philosophy; John E. Page, the Sun Dial; and Lyman Wight, the Wild Ram of the Mountains. They are good men, the best the Lord can find. They will do the will of God, and the Saints know it."[3]

In reference to the president of the Twelve, some say "Brigham Young got the title of 'Lion of the Lord' by his fearless defense of the Prophet Joseph Smith, the gospel, and his dramatic 'roaring' at the pulpit to emphasize a point. After one of his powerful sermons in Nauvoo in 1844, Wilford Woodruff wrote in his diary, 'The Lion roared again tonight.'"[4]

BRIGHAM YOUNG

With this stated, we return to Elder Joseph Fielding Smith's statement that "the matter of succession was properly and rightfully decided." Though this was the case, it must be emphasized that the immediate reorganization of the First Presidency following the death of a president of the Church was not fully enacted by the Twelve Apostles in August 1844, nor would it be fully enacted until September 1898. The process of the reorganization of the First Presidency has come line upon line as the Twelve has asked for direction to guide the Lord's Church.

President Joseph F. Smith explained, "In reality this organization might have been effected within twenty-four hours after the death of the Prophet Joseph Smith, but their action was delayed, until they found by experience that the exercise of the functions of the presidency and the government of the Church by twelve men at the head, was not only cumbersome but was not fully perfect in the order of the Holy Priesthood as established by the Lord."[5]

In a revelation given on January 19, 1841, the Lord designated "Brigham Young to be a president over the Twelve traveling council; Which Twelve hold the keys to open up the authority of my kingdom upon the four corners of the earth" (see D&C 124:127–128). President Young was officially sustained to that position on April 14, 1840.[6] Though President Young served effectively at the head of the Twelve Apostles from that time forward, President Joseph F. Smith noted that he filled the Lord's purposes better as the President of the Church, when the First Presidency was again organized on December 5, 1847, and sustained by the members of the Church on December 27, 1847.[7]

Elder Wilford Woodruff wrote in his journal, dated October 12, 1847, regarding events that led to the first reorganization of the First Presidency. "I had a question put to me by President Young," he wrote. "'What my opinion was concerning one of the Twelve Apostles being appointed as the President of the Church with his two counselors.' I answered that a quorum like the Twelve who had been appointed by revelation, confirmed by revelation from time to time—I thought it would require a revelation to change the order of that quorum. [But] whatever the Lord inspires you to do in this matter. I am with you."[8]

Elder Woodruff's comment must be viewed from the fact that the first organization of the First Presidency in this dispensation never involved a member of the Quorum of the Twelve becoming the president of the Church, or being called as his counselor. It must be remembered that the First Presidency—Joseph Smith as president, and Sidney Rigdon and Frederick G. Williams as first and second counselors—was organized on March 18, 1833.[9] Under the direction of the First Presidency, the three witnesses chose and ordained the first Twelve Apostles in 1835.[10] In addition, based on what was revealed in the revelation on the priesthood (see D&C 107:21–24), and the sustaining vote of the Saints in Nauvoo, the Twelve held authority equal to the First Presidency.[11] Though more than three years had passed since the martyrdom, the Twelve felt no urgency to reorganize the First Presidency.

Providing further insight, Elder Woodruff records a meeting held at Elder Orson Hyde's house. Before Brigham Young was chosen as president of the Church, he wrote:

> Many interesting remarks were made by the various individuals who spoke [this included all the members of the Twelve present], and we were followed by President Young. After which Orson Hyde moved that Brigham Young be the President of the Church of Jesus Christ of Latter-day Saints and that he nominate his two counselors, and they form the First Presidency; seconded by Wilford Woodruff and carried unanimously. President Young nominated Heber C. Kimball as his first counselor; seconded, and carried unanimously. President

Young nominated Willard Richards as his second counselor; seconded, and carried unanimously.[12]

In 1862, President Young presented Elder Woodruff to Isaac Morley and Levi Jackman, saying, "Here is Brother Woodruff, he was the first man that I felt by the spirit to speak to about the organization of the church [meaning: the First Presidency of the Church]."[13]

As noted earlier, President George Q. Cannon of the First Presidency said that through Brigham Young's "unwillingness to push himself forward" to organize the First Presidency, "the Twelve governed the Church for three years."[14] However, his statement in 1862 indicates that he did feel the Spirit move him to reorganize the First Presidency. Following that inspiration, Brother Brigham conversed with his Brethren of the Twelve on the subject, and the reorganization was moved and unanimously carried. Once again the leadership of the Church was fully organized as established by revelation from the Lord.

HEBER C. KIMBALL

Concerning this reorganization, "President [Heber C.] Kimball remarked that himself and Brother Brigham [Young] belonged to the Quorum of the Twelve Apostles, and were no less members of that Quorum on being called to the First Presidency; they are not separated from it now any more than Peter, James, and John were separated from the Quorum of the Twelve when they were called to hold the keys of the Presidency of the Church in their day."[15]

In addition, President Brigham Young said, "Although Brothers Willard Richards, Heber C. Kimball, and myself are out of the Quorum of the Twelve, our Apostleship has not been taken from us. I preached considerable upon this subject in Nauvoo, to give the people the understanding of the different callings of men."[16]

Thus, we learn that from the time of this first reorganization to the present, members of the Twelve who are called into the First Presidency retain their Apostleship. Other men are called and ordained to fill their vacancy in the Quorum of the Twelve. There are usually three members in the First Presidency; there are usually twelve members in the Quorum of the Twelve. These numbers are subject to change, usually by the death of a member of either quorum.

After the death of the Prophet Joseph Smith and his brother Hyrum on June 27, 1844, the Twelve, with Brigham Young at the head, was the First Presidency of the Church. As explained earlier, they were sustained in this position by the members of the Church on August 8, 1844. Therefore, the Twelve served from June 27, 1844, to December 5, 1847—three and a half years. On December 27, 1847, President Brigham Young was sustained by the members of the Church as the president of the Church, at age forty-six. He served effectively for thirty years as the Lord's chosen and designated prophet, seer, and revelator. President Young passed away on August 29, 1877, at age seventy-six.

PRESIDENT JOHN TAYLOR

Less than two months after President Young died, Elder George Q. Cannon gave a sermon on October 8, 1877. During the sermon, he said:

> I have been interrogated upon this point more than any other namely, Who will succeed President Young in case he dies? . . .
>
> Every man who is ordained to the fulness of Apostleship, has the power and the authority to lead and guide the people of God whenever he is called upon to it. . . . And while it is the right of all the Twelve Apostles to receive revelation, and for each one to be a Prophet, to be a Seer, to be a Revelator, and to hold the keys in the fullness, it is only the right of one man at a time to exercise the power in relation to the whole people. . . . The Church is not governed like Zion's Co-operative Institution, by a Board of Directors; this is not God's design. It is governed by men who hold the keys of the Apostleship, who have the right and authority. Any one of them, should an emergency arise, can act as President of the Church, with all the powers, with all the authority, with all the keys, and with every endowment necessary to obtain revelation from God, and to lead and guide this people in the path that leads to the celestial glory; but there is only one man at a time who can hold the keys, who can dictate, who can guide, who can give revelation to the Church.[17]

At that time, that man was President John Taylor, president of the Twelve. He had been sustained to that position on October 6, 1877, two days before Elder Cannon's sermon.[18]

After being designated by revelation (see D&C 118:6), John Taylor was ordained an Apostle on December 19, 1838, at age thirty, under the hands of President Brigham Young, president of the Twelve, and Elder Heber C. Kimball.[19]

On January 26, 1880, Elder Wilford Woodruff received and recorded the following revelation, "I the Lord have raised up . . . my servant John Taylor to preside over you and to be a Law giver unto my Church. He has mingled his blood with that of the martyred prophets. Nevertheless,

John Taylor

while I have taken my servants Joseph and Hyrum Smith unto myself, I have preserved my servant John Taylor for a wise purpose in me. I have also taken many others of the Apostles unto myself; for I take whom I will take and preserve in life those whom I will preserve, according to . . . my will."[20]

Being in tune with the Spirit, Elder Woodruff was further instructed, "While my servant John Taylor is your President, I wish to ask the rest of my servants of the Apostles the question: Although you have one to preside over your quorum and over the Church which is the order of God in all generations, do you not all of you hold the Apostleship which is the highest authority ever given to man on the earth? You do. Therefore, you hold in common the keys of the kingdom in all the world. Each of you have power to unlock the veil of eternity and hold converse with God the Father and his son Jesus Christ and to have the administration of angels."[21]

In addition to this revelation, President George Q. Cannon of the First Presidency wrote:

> For some years attention was not called to the proper arrangement of the names of the Twelve; but some time before President Young's death, they were arranged by him in their proper order. Not long before his death, a number of the Twelve and leading Elders were in Sanpete [Utah] when, in the presence of the congregation in the meetinghouse, he turned to President Taylor, and said, 'Here is the man whose right it is to preside over the council in my absence, he being the senior apostle.'
>
> Therefore, as I have said, when President Young died there was no doubt . . . who was the man—it was the

then senior Apostle. He was the man who had the right to preside, he holding the keys by virtue of his seniority, by virtue of his position in the Quorum; and he became the President of the Twelve Apostles; and became President of the Church.[22]

After the death of President Brigham Young on August 29, 1877, the Twelve, with President John Taylor at the head, was the First Presidency of the Church. They served from August 29, 1877, to October 10, 1880—a three-year period. President Taylor was sustained as the president of the Church on October 10, 1880, at age seventy-one. "The First Presidency was again reorganized with John Taylor as President of the Church, and George Q. Cannon and Joseph F. Smith as his first and second counselor, respectively."[23] President Taylor served effectively for seven years. He passed away on July 25, 1887, at age seventy-eight.[24]

PRESIDENT WILFORD WOODRUFF

Concerning President Taylor's death, Elder Wilford Woodruff wrote the following correspondence:

> As I was going to bed I received the telegraphic dispatch saying President Taylor was dead. I did not sleep much that night. . . . Arrived in S L City [Utah] at 10 0'clock. Spent the day in the President's Office. Met some apostles and others. This was on the 28th [of July, 1887]. On the 29th of July the funeral was held at the tabernacle at 12 o' clock, but the night before I went to the Gardo House and viewed the body of President Taylor. I met the next day with G. Q. Cannon and Joseph F. Smith and the Apostles, and President George Q. Cannon [First Counselor to President Taylor] surrendered into the hands of the Quorum of the Twelve Apostles the power and authority of the business of the Church.[25]

President Cannon's action is an important practice of the Church. When a president of the Church dies, the Apostles preside. President Cannon resumed the place in the Quorum of the Twelve that he had occupied before he served as a counselor. President Joseph F. Smith did the same. The Twelve Apostles once again became the First Presidency of the Church.

Designated by revelation (see D&C 118:6), Elder Wilford Woodruff, at age thirty-two, was ordained an Apostle on April 26, 1839, by President Brigham Young, then president of the Twelve.[26] When President Taylor was sustained as president of the Church on October 10, 1880, Elder Woodruff was sustained that same day as the president of the Quorum of the Twelve Apostles.[27]

Then, as Elder Joseph Fielding Smith wrote:

> Following the death of President Taylor the duty of presidency again devolved upon the council of the apostles, Counselors Cannon and Smith resuming their places with the Twelve. The apostles continued to act in that position until the April Conference in 1889, when the First Presidency was again organized with Wilford Woodruff as President. He selected George Q. Cannon and Joseph F. Smith as his counselors. At the time of this organization President Woodruff was 82 years of age, but hale and vigorous.[28]

Therefore, after the death of President John Taylor on July 25, 1887, the Twelve, with President Wilford Woodruff at the head, was the First Presidency of the Church. They served from July 25, 1887, to April 7, 1889—two years. President Woodruff was then sustained as president of the Church on April 7, 1889, at age eighty-two. He served effectively for nine and a half years. He passed away on September 2, 1898, at age ninety-one.

Reiterating doctrines that have been explained earlier, President George Q. Cannon, first counselor to President Wilford Woodruff, said, "President Woodruff is the only man upon the earth who holds the keys of the sealing power. These apostles all around me have all the same authority that he has. We are all ordained with the same ordination. We all have had the same keys and the same powers bestowed upon us. [Note these next words:] But there is an order in the Church of God, and that order is that there is only one man at a time on the earth that holds the keys of sealing, and that man is the President of the Church, now Wilford Woodruff."[29]

In addition to the sealing keys, each Apostle holds all the powers, all the authority, all the keys, and all the right to preside and administer the affairs of the Lord's Church. However, there is an order in the Church: the senior Apostle has the right to preside over and direct his fellow Apostles. This is a critical doctrine of the Church.

Two days before President Woodruff was sustained as president of the Church, he met with the Brethren of the Twelve and told them the Lord had that it was right for the Brethren to organize the First Presidency. He also noted that it was the mind and will of the Lord that Brothers George Q. Cannon and Joseph F. Smith be his counselors. After discussion and sustaining by the members of the Twelve, the First Presidency was organized.[30]

From this information, we learn how the First Presidency was organized on April 5, 1889. Two days later, Wilford Woodruff was sustained as president of the Church by the general Church membership, with George Q. Cannon and Joseph F. Smith sustained as his first and second counselors.

PRESIDENT LORENZO SNOW

After the death of President Wilford Woodruff on September 2, 1898, the Twelve, with President Lorenzo Snow at the head, was the First Presidency of the Church for only eleven days. President Snow was ordained and set apart as president of the Church on September 13, 1898, at age eighty-four. As Elder Joseph Fielding Smith explained, "The reason for this immediate action in reorganizing the First Presidency was a statement by President Woodruff, shortly before his death, that 'it was not the will of the Lord that in the future there should be a lengthy period elapse between the death of the president and the re-organization of the Presidency.'"[31]

LORENZO SNOW

President Snow served effectively for three years. He passed away on October 10, 1901, at age eighty-seven.

DAYS THE TWELVE WERE THE FIRST PRESIDENCY

The Twelve serve as the First Presidency of the Church after the death of a president of the Church. Following are the specific number of days the Twelve served in this position:

- 1,256 days—President Brigham Young was ordained and set apart as president of the Church on December 5, 1847. He served until August 29, 1877.
- 1,137 days—President John Taylor was sustained as the president of the Church on October 10, 1880. He served until July 25, 1887.
- 621 days—President Wilford Woodruff was sustained as the president of the Church on April 7, 1889. He served until September 2, 1898.
- 11 days—President Lorenzo Snow was ordained and set apart as the president of the Church on September 13, 1898. He served until October 10, 1901.
- 7 days—President Joseph F. Smith was ordained and set apart as president of the Church on October 17, 1901. He served until November 19, 1918.
- 4 days—President Heber J. Grant was ordained and set apart as president of the Church on November 23, 1918. He served until May 14, 1945.
- 7 days—President George Albert Smith was ordained and set apart as president of the Church on May 21, 1945. He served until April 4, 1951.
- 5 days—President David O. McKay was ordained and set apart as president of the Church on April 9, 1951. He served until January 18, 1970.
- 5 days—President Joseph Fielding Smith was ordained and set apart as president of the Church on January 23, 1970. He served until July 2, 1972.
- 5 days—President Harold B. Lee was ordained and set apart as president of the Church on July 7, 1972. He served until December 26, 1973.
- 4 days—President Spencer W. Kimball was ordained and set apart as president of the Church on December. 30, 1973. He served until November 5, 1985.
- 5 days—President Ezra Taft Benson was ordained and set apart as president of the Church on November 10, 1985. He served until May 30, 1994.

- 7 days—President Howard W. Hunter was ordained and set apart as president of the Church on June 5, 1994. He served until March 3, 1995.
- 9 days—President Gordon B. Hinckley was ordained and set apart as president of the Church on March 12, 1995. He serves to this day.[32]

The immediate reorganization of the First Presidency following the death of a president of the Church was not fully enacted by the Twelve Apostles in August 1844; in fact, the process was not fully enacted until September 13, 1898, when President Lorenzo Snow was ordained and sustained as president of the Church. The time of the Twelve being the First Presidency has decreased from three and one half years in President Young's era to nearly a week in our day.

GEORGE Q. CANNON, WILFORD WOODRUFF, AND JOSEPH F. SMITH.

CHAPTER 9

APOSTLES NOT OF THE TWELVE

MEMBERS OF THE FIRST PRESIDENCY

As explained earlier, members of the Quorum of the Twelve Apostles who are called into the First Presidency retain their Apostleship and seniority.[1] However, there have been members of the First Presidency who were not ordained an Apostle. Likewise, there have been members of the First Presidency who have been ordained an Apostle but never served as a member of the Quorum of the Twelve Apostles.

President Joseph F. Smith wrote, "We have the council of the first presidency consisting of three presiding high priests who are called of God and appointed to preside over the Church and over the Priesthood of God, and I want to say here that it does not follow and never has followed that the members of the First Presidency of the Church are necessarily to be ordained Apostles."[2]

As a member of the First Presidency, President Smith knew that the senior Apostle always becomes president of the Church. Therefore, there will at least be one Apostle in the First Presidency. The counselors, if not Apostles, are given the keys by ordination. President Smith writes:

> It was stated that several persons who acted as counselors in the First Presidency had never been ordained apostles. Several correspondents have objected to the statement that Sidney Rigdon, Jedediah M. Grant, Daniel H. Wells, John R. Winder, and others were not ordained

apostles. We still maintain, upon lack of convincing evidence to the contrary, that none of these brethren was ever ordained an apostle. We do know positively that John R. Winder, Sidney Rigdon, William Law and Hyrum Smith, all of whom were members in the First Presidency of the Church, were never ordained apostles. But, be that as it may, however, the main point we wish to make is this, that it was not necessary that they should be so ordained apostles in order to hold the position of counselor in the First Presidency. The leading fact to be remembered is that the Priesthood is greater than any of its offices; and that any man holding the Melchizedek Priesthood may, by virtue of its possession, perform any ordinance pertaining thereto, or connected therewith, when called upon to do so by one holding the proper authority, which proper authority is vested in the President of the Church, or in any whom he may designate.[3]

President Joseph F. Smith's statement in regards to Sidney Rigdon is substantiated by what is written in *Essentials in Church History* (page 687) and the *2001–2002 Church Almanac* (page 57).

Essentials in Church History (page 690) doesn't record whether Jedediah M. Grant, second counselor to President Young, was ordained an Apostle. However, the *Church Almanac* (page 60) notes that he was ordained an Apostle on April 7, 1854, by President Brigham Young, and sustained as second counselor the same day. Therefore, we must determine the validity of what is written.

Essentials in Church History (page 690) records that Daniel H. Wells, second counselor to President Young, was ordained an Apostle and set apart as second counselor on January 4, 1857, by President Brigham Young. However, the *Church Almanac* (page 60) doesn't record whether he was ordained an Apostle the day he was set apart as second counselor. Again, we must determine the validity.

Both *Essentials in Church History* (page 688) and the *Church Almanac* (page 57) verify that John R. Winder, first counselor to President Joseph F. Smith, was not ordained an Apostle.

Essentials in Church History (page 690) and the *Church Almanac* (page 59) both also support that William Law, second counselor to President Joseph Smith, was not ordained an Apostle.

Elder Joseph Fielding Smith made the following observation about Hyrum Smith, brother of the prophet, and Oliver Cowdery:

> It was Oliver Cowdery . . . who knelt with the Prophet Joseph at the altar in the Kirtland Temple, April 3, 1836, when the Savior, Moses, Elias, Elijah, and perhaps other ancient prophets came and conferred with them, bestowing keys, Priesthood, and authority of former dispensations. . . . All these blessings Oliver Cowdery would have held throughout eternity if he had remained faithful and true to his calling; but he fell away, and therefore the Lord bestowed these gifts, blessings and powers of presidency, upon the head of Hyrum Smith, the faithful brother of the Prophet Joseph. . . .
>
> Sunday, January 24, 1841, Hyrum Smith received the ordinations to these holy callings under the hands of President Joseph Smith.[4]

The *Church Almanac* (pages 56–57) records this about Hyrum: "Given all the priesthood formerly held by Oliver Cowdery (including apostle); ordained Patriarch to the Church and assistant president January 24, 1841, by Joseph Smith."

As already noted in chapter 3, Elder Joseph Fielding Smith said:

> In the Doctrine and Covenants, section 27:12–13, the Lord says that he sent Peter, James, and John to ordain Joseph Smith and Oliver Cowdery and that by virtue of that ordination they became Apostles and special witnesses. This is true, but . . . these men were not ordained to the specific office in the priesthood, but received the priesthood itself out of which the offices come. Joseph Smith and Oliver Cowdery were therefore, by virtue of the conferring of priesthood, Apostles or special witnesses, for Jesus Christ.[5]

Though Hyrum Smith received the ordinations previously held by Oliver Cowdery, Elder Joseph Fielding Smith's statement supports the remarks made by President Joseph F. Smith that Hyrum Smith was never ordained an Apostle. If some of the men we've named were ordained an

Apostle, that ordination was similar to that of Joseph Smith and Oliver Cowdery—special witnesses for Jesus Christ.

PRESIDENT YOUNG ORDAINED HIS SONS

We now turn to an April 17, 1864 meeting, which was attended by President Brigham Young and Elders John Taylor and George A. Smith of the Twelve, who met for prayer. President Young told these Brethren that he had ordained his sons, Joseph A., Brigham Young Jr., and John W. as Apostles and as his counselors. President Young explained that by ordaining his sons, he could put his sons into active service in the spiritual affairs of the kingdom.[6]

JOHN W. YOUNG

A week later, on April 24, Elder Wilford Woodruff wrote: "President Young and [Heber C.] Kimball set apart D[aniel]. H. Wells, Brigham Young, Jr. and Orson Pratt for their missions. President Young said I have ordained my son Brigham unto all the priesthood and power that I hold myelf and appointed him one of my counselors, and now Brother Kimball you bless him if you feel like it. Then Brother Kimball gave him a good blessing."[7]

Joseph Angell Young, at age twenty-nine, Brigham Young Jr., at age twenty-seven, and John Willard Young, at age nineteen, were ordained Apostles on February 4, 1864, by their father, President Brigham Young. However, none of these three men were members of the Twelve.

Elder George A. Smith was called out of the Twelve and sustained to fill the vacancy that resulted after the death of President Heber C. Kimball, first counselor to President Young. Brigham Young Jr. was called to fill Elder Smith's vacancy. This was on October 9, 1868, four and a half years after being ordained an Apostle by his father. Elder Brigham Young Jr. was sustained as a counselor to President Young on April 8, 1873; sustained as assistant counselor on May 9, 1874; released at the death of his father, wherein he resumed his position in the Twelve; and sustained president of the Quorum of the Twelve on October 17, 1901. He died on April 11, 1903, at age sixty-six.

No official Church record says that Joseph A. Young was sustained as a counselor to President Young. Brother Joseph A. Young died August 5, 1875, at age forty.

John W. Young was sustained as a counselor to President Young on April 8, 1873; sustained as assistant counselor on May 9, 1874; sustained as first counselor on October 7, 1876. He was released at the death of his father; sustained as a counselor to the Twelve on October 6, 1877; was released on October 6, 1891. He died on February 11, 1924, at age seventy-nine.[8]

JOSEPH F. SMITH

Our attention is now turned to Joseph Fielding Smith, who is commonly referred to as Joseph F. Smith. He was ordained an Apostle by President Brigham Young on July 1, 1866, and was immediately named as a counselor in the First Presidency, at age twenty-seven.[9]

Over a year later, the "October Conference of the Church in 1867 was held in the new Tabernacle, which was nearing completion.... He serves Elder Joseph F. Smith, son of Patriarch Hyrum Smith was called to fill a vacancy in the council of the twelve, caused by the apostasy of Amasa M. Lyman."[10]

Under various presidents of the Church, Elder Smith served as second and first counselor. He was ordained and set apart as the president of the Church on October 17, 1901, at age sixty-two; he passed away on November 19, 1918, at age eighty.[11]

ALBERT CARRINGTON

Albert Carrington, age fifty-seven, was ordained an Apostle on July 3, 1870, by President Brigham Young. He was sustained as a counselor to President Young on April 8, 1873 and was assistant counselor to President Young on May 9, 1874. He was released at the death of President Young on August 29, 1877. He was excommunicated from the Church on November 7, 1885; however, he was baptized again on November 1, 1887. He passed away on September 19, 1889, at age seventy-six.[12]

COUNSELOR TO THE TWELVE

As written earlier, Daniel H. Wells was set apart on January 4, 1857, as second counselor to President Brigham Young. Twenty years later, he was sustained as a counselor to the Twelve Apostles on October 6, 1877.[13] John W. Young, a son of President Brigham Young, was sustained as a counselor to his father on April 8, 1873. Four years later, he, too, was sustained as a counselor to the Twelve Apostles on the same day as was Daniel H. Wells.[14]

At a general conference held on April 5, 1890, the authorities were presented for the votes of the assembly.

"Wilford Woodruff as Prophet, Seer, and Revelator, and President of The Church of Jesus Christ of Latter-day Saints in all the world.

"George Q. Cannon as first counselor in the First Presidency. Joseph F. Smith as Second Counselor in the First Presidency.

"Lorenzo Snow as President of the Twelve Apostles.

"As members of the Council of the Twelve Apostles—Lorenzo Snow, Franklin D. Richards, Brigham Young [Jr.], Moses Thatcher, Francis M. Lyman, John H. Smith, George Teasdale, Heber J. Grant, John W. Taylor, Marriner W. Merrill, Anton H. Lund, and Abraham H. Cannon.

"Counselors to the Twelve Apostles—John W. Young and Daniel H. Wells."[15]

Note the words "Counselors in the First Presidency, and the Twelve Apostles with their counselors, as Prophets, Seers, and Revelators" and "Patriarch to the Church—John Smith."

This means that Daniel H. Wells and John W. Young were sustained at this April 1890 general conference as prophet, seers, and revelators. Today, only the President of the Church and his counselors in the First Presidency and the Twelve Apostles are sustained as prophet, seers, and revelators.

In a personal letter dated October 20, 2004, the following information was furnished by the Family and Church History Department:

"Thank you for your request for information about the calling of Counselor and Associate for the Quorum of the Twelve Apostles. Daniel Wells was called as a Counselor to the Twelve from October 6, 1877, until his death March 24, 1891. During this time he was called to serve in the British Mission (1884) and later President of the Manti Temple (1888).

"John Willard Young was ordained an Apostle (not in the Quorum of the Twelve) 4 February 1864; . . . sustained as a counselor to the Twelve Apostles 6 October 1877 to 6 October 1891."[16]

Records indicate that Brother Young "requested that his name be no longer presented" as a counselor to the Twelve.[17] Accordingly, he was released at the October 1891 general conference. He passed away on February 11, 1924, at age seventy-nine.[18] Using the dates above for calculations,

Daniel H. Wells served for thirteen and a half years as a counselor to the Twelve; John W. Young served for fourteen years.

ASSOCIATE TO THE TWELVE

The April 1938 Conference Report, notes "Sylvester Q. Cannon to be ordained an Apostle of the Lord Jesus Christ, and to be set apart as an associate of the Council of the Twelve Apostles."[19]

In an address at a Relief Society Conference, President David O. McKay said:

> The point I am making is that a man may be an apostle but not one of the Council of the Twelve. We have had that in our day. John W. Young was ordained an apostle February 4, 1864, but he was never a member of the Council of the Twelve from that time to the day of his death. . . . Brigham Young, Jr., was ordained as an apostle by his father on February 4, 1864, but he did not become a member of the Council of the Twelve until October 1868, when he was chosen to fill the vacancy caused by George A. Smith. Today Brother Sylvester Q. Cannon has been ordained an apostle, but is not sustained as a member of the Council of the Twelve.[20]

The letter from the Family and Church History Department also notes, "Sylvester Quayle Cannon was sustained as Associate to the Quorum of the Twelve Apostles 6 April 1938. He was ordained an apostle (not in the Quorum of the Twelve) 14 April 1938 and sustained to the Quorum of the Twelve Apostles 6 October 1939.

"The research I have done does not show any special reason for the difference in terminology between Counselor and Associate to the Quorum of the Twelve Apostles. It is possible that the presiding authorities were called to fill a need which the President of the Church or Quorum of the Twelve had for help in administering the Church and just used the terms as they saw fit."

Previous to being ordained an Apostle, Brother Cannon was sustained as the Presiding Bishop of the Church on June 4, 1925. He then was ordained an Apostle by President Heber J. Grant. After being sustained as a member of the Quorum of the Twelve Apostles on October 6,

1939, at age sixty-two, Elder Cannon served until he passed away on May 29, 1943, at age sixty-five.[21]

ALVIN R. DYER

The last man in this dispensation to be ordained an Apostle but not sustained as a member of the Quorum of the Twelve Apostles was Alvin R. Dyer. The September 1967 Conference Report records that "Elder Alvin R. Dyer, an assistant to the Twelve, was sustained at this conference to be an Apostle."[22]

At that same general conference, Elder Dyer noted:

> When President McKay asked me in the [Salt Lake] temple a few days ago if I would accept the calling of the apostleship, I replied that I would, although I was somewhat perplexed as to what the calling would mean under the circumstances. As we moved to another room in the temple, my feelings were somewhat quieted by the kind and meaningful words of a member of the Quorum of the Twelve, whom I greatly love and respect. After extending his well wishes, he said these words (and they have tremendous meaning): "Don't worry, Alvin. You have been called by the highest authority upon the earth to this calling, and it will be made known to you what you are to do."
>
> I know only partially now, at the present time, what holding the apostleship in my case will entail for me. I know, of course, that the Lord has made known that an apostle is to contend against none but the church of evil, to take upon himself the name of Christ and speak the truth in soberness, and to be a witness, a special witness for Jesus Christ in the world.[23]

After being sustained, Elder Dyer was ordained an Apostle on October 5, 1967, at age sixty-four, by President David O. McKay. He was sustained as a counselor in the First Presidency on April 6, 1968, and released at the death of President McKay on January 18, 1970. Elder Dyer then resumed his position as assistant to the Twelve Apostles on January 23, 1970. He was sustained as a member of the First Quorum of the Seventy on October 1, 1976. He passed away on March 6, 1977, at age seventy-four.[24]

From what has been presented, we know that men have been ordained Apostles and called to serve as counselors in the First Presidency. We have further learned that counselors in the First Presidency are not necessarily ordained Apostles. Men have been called and sustained as counselor and associate for the Quorum of the Twelve Apostles yet not set apart as Apostles. Lastly, the reverse is also true; men have been ordained an Apostle but never been sustained as a member of the Quorum of the Twelve Apostles. Why? "To fill a need which the President of the Church or the Quorum of the Twelve had for help in administering the Church" (see letter from Family and Church History Department).

The full organization of the Church was not revealed at the beginning. It has came line upon line as our leaders have asked for direction. It is important to realize that calls to serve in the leading councils of the Church come by revelation or inspiration to the president of the Church. He is the one who issues the call for the Lord. Our duty is to sustain those who have been called by the Lord's chosen servant.

CHAPTER 10
THE TWELVE SPEAK ABOUT THEIR CALLING

BLESSINGS, PREDICTIONS, AND IMPRESSIONS

Various members of the Twelve have related personal information about their call to the Apostleship. Some were surprised by their calling, but many were informed either by a blessing, a prediction, or an impression that they would be called.

WILFORD WOODRUFF
ORDAINED APOSTLE ON APRIL 26, 1839

President Wilford Woodruff was the fourth president of the Church and the father of Elder Abraham O. Woodruff of the Twelve. Elder Wilford Woodruff wrote the following about his call to the Twelve:

> "While holding meeting with the Saints at North Vinal Haven, on the 9th of August [1838], I received a letter from Elder Thomas B. Marsh, who was then President of the Twelve Apostles, informing me that the Prophet Joseph Smith had received a revelation from the Lord [D&C 118:6], naming as persons to be chosen to fill the places of those of the Twelve who had fallen. Those named were John E. Page, John Taylor, Wilford Woodruff and Willard Richards.... The substance of this letter had been revealed to me several weeks before, but I had not named it to any person."

It was on the 8th of July, just one week after Wilford's

memorable experience at his father's home, that this humble, faithful, diligent elder was called by the voice of God, through His Prophet, to be one of the Twelve Apostles of the Lamb in this dispensation; and Wilford being at the time many hundreds of miles distant from the Prophet, the Lord then revealed to him the fact of that calling.[1]

Wilford Woodruff was ordained an Apostle on April 26, 1839, at age thirty-two, by President Brigham Young; he was sustained as president of the Quorum of the Twelve Apostles on October 10, 1880. He was sustained as president of the Church on April 7, 1889, at age eighty-two. He passed away on September 2, 1898, at age ninety-one.[2]

GEORGE A. SMITH
ORDAINED APOSTLE ON APRIL 26, 1839

Elder George A. Smith is the father of Elder John Henry Smith of the Twelve and the grandfather of President George Albert Smith, eighth president of the Church. In his personal journal, he wrote:

> I was born at Pottsdam, St. Lawrence County, New York, June 26, 1817. My father, John Smith, was the sixth son of Asael and Mary, and was born July 16, 1781.
>
> 1827: The winter after I was 9 years old, I received a blow upon my head, which rendered me insensible for three weeks; a council of surgeons decided that the skull was fractured, and the blood settled under it, and that the only remedy was trepanning [using a surgical instrument to remove a section of the skull]. My father, being a man of faith, and believing that God would heal me, dismissed the physicians, and in a few weeks I recovered, although for many years I felt the effects of that blow.
>
> At an early age I felt a disposition to enquire after the original principles of the Gospel.
>
> 1830: In the month of August, 1830, my uncle, Joseph Smith [the father of the Prophet Joseph Smith] and his youngest son, Don Carlos, came to my father's [home] on a visit, bringing with them some Books of Mormon . . . .

My mother and myself [age 13] occupied Saturday and Sunday reading the Book of Mormon. . . .

I continued to read the Book of Mormon and framed in my mind a series of objections, which I supposed were sufficient to overthrow its authenticity, and on the return of my Uncle Joseph, I undertook to argue with him upon the subject, but he so successfully removed my objections and enlightened my mind that I have never since ceased to advocate the divine authenticity of that book.

1839: In the latter part of January, [the Prophet] Joseph sent me word by [his brother] Don Carlos Smith that I was appointed to be one of the Twelve Apostles. . . . About the first of February I ascertained by accident that Brothers Brigham Young and Heber C. Kimball were going to Liberty to visit the prisoners. As they mounted their horses I joined them and asked permission to accompany them, which was readily granted. I had felt very timid about conversing or making myself familiar with any of the Twelve, as Lyman E. Johnson, John Boynton and some others, who formerly belonged to the Quorum, had treated me rather aristocratically, which, added to the high respect I had for their calling, made me feel embarrassed in their presence; and I felt delicate about asking them [Elders Young and Kimball] for the privilege of accompanying them. On the way, Brother Kimball told me I was named to be one of the Twelve. . . .

We traveled . . . to Liberty. . . . Judge Tillery, the jailer, permitted us to go in and see the prisoners. We were locked in with them for about an hour. [My cousin, the Prophet] Joseph told me of my calling to the Apostleship and enquired how I liked it. I replied. "I was pleased with the appointment, and would do my best to honor it."[3]

George A. Smith was ordained an Apostle on April 26, 1839, at age twenty-one by Heber C. Kimball. He was sustained as first counselor to President Brigham Young on October 7, 1868. He passed away on September 1, 1875, at age fifty-eight.[4]

Franklin Dewey Richards
ORDAINED APOSTLE ON FEBRUARY 12, 1849

Elder Franklin D. Richards is the father of Elder George F. Richards of the Twelve and the grandfather of Elder LeGrand Richards of the Twelve. In his journal, dated August 13, 1847, he wrote:

> This morning I awoke from a dream in which I seemed to have been with President Brigham Young in the Temple at Nauvoo. We sat opposite each other, with our feet in a clear, lively pool of water, and we conversed together. He asked, "Brother Franklin, would you accept it if I should appoint you one of the Quorum [of the Twelve]?" I replied, "Brother Brigham, I always have accepted, and as far as I could, have obeyed every appointment that has been given to me, and I always intend to." He then showed me several books containing peculiar drawings and diagrams, many of which were lightly colored and in the Prophet Joseph's own hand writing. While I was examining the books I awoke, and felt as happy as if I had really been in the company of President Young, and the holy influence seemed to rest upon my whole person.[5]

The following was related by President Lorenzo Snow:

> I want to relate one circumstance . . . before I close. I would not tell it if it concerned myself alone. In the days of the "reformation," when President Young was aroused to call upon the people to repent and reform, he talked very strongly as to what ought to be done with some people—that their Priesthood ought to be taken from them, because of their failure to magnify it as they should have done. The brethren who lived in those days will remember how vigorously he spoke in this direction. Well, it touched Brother Franklin's [D. Richards] heart, and it touched mine also; and we talked the matter over to ourselves. [As members of the Twelve] We concluded we would go to President Young and offer him our Priesthood, if he felt in the name of the Lord that we had not

magnified our Priesthood, we would resign it. We went to him, saw him alone, and told him this. I guess there were tears in his eyes when he said, "Brother Lorenzo, Brother Franklin, you have magnified your Priesthood satisfactorily to the Lord. God bless you."[6]

Franklin D. Richards was ordained an Apostle on February 12, 1849, at age twenty-seven, by Heber C. Kimball; he was sustained as president of the Quorum of the Twelve Apostles on September 13, 1898. He passed away on December 9, 1899, at age seventy-eight.[7]

GEORGE Q. CANNON
ORDAINED APOSTLE ON AUGUST 26, 1860

Elder Cannon's story follows:

George Q. Cannon

After completing his Hawaiian mission, while returning home in 1854, Elder Cannon tarried some time in California working with Elder Parley P. Pratt on his autobiography, that vivid account of the early scenes of the Church and the participation of the eloquent apostle in them. During that close companionship, the older man developed a strong friendship for the youth who had done such a remarkable work among the Hawaiians. On one occasion the spirit of prophecy rested on Elder Pratt and he predicted that George Q. Cannon would succeed him as a member of the Council of the Twelve. The vigorous Brother Pratt was then entering middle age and it appeared that his life would be prolonged many years. However, at the age of fifty, less than three years from the time of the prophecy, he was assassinated in Arkansas. It was, therefore, not a surprise to Elder Cannon, who had kept the prediction secret, that he was called October 23, 1859, to fill his place. More than two years had passed since Elder Pratt's death without action being taken. George Q. Cannon was then thirty-two years old.[8]

In addition to this inspired prediction given by Elder Pratt, Elder Cannon revealed the following:

It is a very responsible station for a man to stand as an Apostle of the Lord Jesus Christ, to stand as one upon whom the responsibility rests of counseling the people, of directing them and of imparting to them such instructions as are needed by them; and I naturally shrink from this responsibility. I never did desire prominence among men. The Lord revealed to me when I was quite young that I at some time would be an Apostle. I never told it to any human being; but on more than one occasion I have gone out and besought the Lord to choose some one else, and to relieve me of that responsibility. I have besought him earnestly, time and again, that if I could only get my salvation and exaltation without being called to that high and holy responsibility, I would much rather He would choose some other person. These have always been my feelings concerning responsibility in this Church; yet I have endeavored to the best of my ability when responsibility has been placed upon me to bear it off, with the help of God, the best I could.[9]

Seven years later, Elder Cannon also noted that "God has chosen us expressly for . . . this work, and we cannot get out of it. Personally I tried to get out of this responsibility. The Lord revealed to me in my youth that I was to be an Apostle, . . . I besought Him that He would not choose me to hold this office, for I had seen what I would have to go through, and I shrunk from it. But we are chosen, and we cannot get out of it honorably."[10]

After serving as an Apostle for nearly twenty-one years, Elder Cannon was called as a counselor in the First Presidency. Regarding this new opportunity, he wrote, "Before the names of the counselors [to President John Taylor] were called, I had a presentiment that my name would be mentioned, and I trembled all over. My nerves twitched all over my body, and I could scarcely control myself. When my name was mentioned, I rose to my feet and begged of the brethren to excuse me from filling that position. I told them that I would much rather remain in the Quorum of the Twelve. . . . President Taylor said it was not a matter of personal choice."[11]

George Q. Cannon was ordained an Apostle on August 26, 1860, at age thirty-three, by President Brigham Young. He was sustained as a counselor to President Young on April 8, 1873; sustained as assistant counselor to President Young on May 9, 1874; released at the death of President Young on August 29, 1877. He was sustained as first counselor to President John Taylor on October 10, 1880; released at the death of President Taylor on July 25, 1887; sustained as first counselor to President Wilford Woodruff on April 7, 1889; sustained as first counselor to President Lorenzo Snow on September 13, 1898. He passed away on April 12, 1901, at age seventy-four.[12]

JOSEPH F. SMITH
ORDAINED APOSTLE ON JULY 1, 1866

President Joseph F. Smith, sixth president of the Church, is the father of Elders Hyrum Mack Smith and Joseph Fielding Smith, of the Twelve. The following records his calling:

JOSEPH F. SMITH

> On the first of July [1866], . . . he [Wilford Woodruff] makes this record, respecting the words of President Young at the close of a prayer circle which had just been held by the Presidency and some of the brethren. As they were about to leave, President Young spoke up: "Hold on. Shall I do as I feel led to do? I always feel well when I follow the promptings of the spirit. It has come to my mind to ordain Brother Joseph F. Smith to the Apostleship, and to be one of my counselors." He then called upon each one of us for an expression of our feelings and we responded with our hearty approval. Joseph F. Smith was then ordained under the hands of Brigham Young and the brethren present to be an Apostle in The Church of Jesus Christ of Latter-day Saints and to be a special witness to the nations of the earth. He was further ordained to be a counselor in the First Presidency of the Church.[13]

Elder Joseph Fielding Smith, a son of Joseph F. Smith, provides additional information concerning this meeting:

> July 1, 1866, Joseph F. Smith met with President Brigham Young and a number of the Apostles in the

upper room in the Historian's Office, in a council and prayer meeting according to the custom of the presiding brethren; Joseph F. was the secretary to this council. After the close of the prayer circle, President Brigham Young suddenly turned to his brethren and said, "Hold on, shall I do as I feel lead? I always feel well to do as the Spirit constrains me. It is my mind to ordain Brother Joseph F. Smith to the Apostleship, and to be one of my counselors." He then called upon each of the brethren present for an expression of their feelings, and each responded individually stating that such action met with their hearty approval. The brethren then laid their hands upon the head of Joseph F., and President Young who was voice said: "Brother Joseph F. Smith, we lay our hands upon your head in the name of Jesus Christ, and by virtue of the Holy Priesthood we ordain you to be an Apostle in The Church of Jesus Christ of Latter-day Saints, and to be a special witness to the nations of the earth. We seal upon your head all the authority, power and keys of this holy Apostleship; and we ordain you to be a counselor to the First Presidency of the Church and Kingdom of God upon the earth. These blessings we seal upon you in the name of Jesus Christ and by the authority of the Holy Priesthood. Amen."

After the ordination President Young declared that he did not wish in the recording of this blessing to lead anyone to suppose that this mode was the only way in which such an ordination could be performed. He also admonished the brethren to keep the fact of this ordination to themselves, for it was wisdom that it should not be revealed at that time, although it should be recorded.[14]

Later, he continued his explanation, writing, "In this calling Joseph F. Smith served without the matter having been made public until the October general conference of 1867, when on Tuesday, the 8th, he was sustained as a member of the Council of the Twelve Apostles, succeeding Amasa M. Lyman."[15]

Therefore, Joseph F. Smith served as an Apostle and a counselor for one year, three months, and seven days after his ordination without the membership of the Church knowing. Evidently the Spirit told President Young not to reveal this information.

Then, thirteen years after Joseph F. Smith was publicly sustained as a member of the Twelve, Elder Wilford Woodruff made the following prophecy:

> The Quarterly Conference there [in Ogden, Utah], convened on the 22nd and 23rd [of January, 1881], and it was on this occasion, after an address to the people by [Elder] Joseph F. Smith, that Elder Woodruff arose and prophesied that the man to whom they [the congregation] had just listened would yet become the President of the Church in all the world. In his journal he asks that the prophecy be made a note of, and that it be made a matter of special record when its fulfillment was realized, which was October 17th, 1901, more than twenty and a half years after the prophecy was uttered, and more than thirty years from the time he made the same prediction in Nephi [Utah].
>
> "NEPHI, March 22nd, 1909.
>
> "About the year 1869, two apostles visited Nephi and held [a] meeting there. They were Wilford Woodruff and Joseph F. Smith. On Sunday morning they attended Sunday School, which was held in the old Social Hall. Elder Woodruff interested the children by speaking of incidents in the life of the Prophet Joseph Smith and of his labors. He then turned to Elder Joseph F. Smith and asked him to arise to his feet. Elder Smith complied. 'Look at him, children,' Wilford Woodruff said, 'for he resembles the Prophet Joseph more than any man living. He will become the President of The Church of Jesus Christ of Latter-day Saints. I want you, every one of you, to remember what I have told you this morning. After this Brother Woodruff called on Elder Smith to speak. The latter said he could remember the Prophet, although he was then very young. He remembered sitting upon his knees. I was present on this occasion.
>
> "Respectfully, Langley A. Bailey."[16]

In addition to this statement, President Grant revealed the following:

Lorenzo Snow was drowned in the harbor of Honolulu, in the Hawaiian Islands, and it took some hours to bring him to life again. At that particular time the Lord revealed to him the fact that the young man Joseph F. Smith, who had refused to get off the vessel that had carried them from San Francisco to Honolulu [March, 1864], and get into a small boat, would some day be the Prophet of God. [In] answering Lorenzo Snow who was in charge of the company, [Joseph F.] said: "If you by the authority of the Priesthood of God, which you hold, tell me to get into that boat and attempt to land, I will do so, but unless you command me in the authority of the Priesthood, I will not do so, because it is not safe to attempt to land in a small boat while this typhoon is raging." They laughed at the young man Joseph F. Smith, but he said, "The boat will capsize." The others got into the boat, and it did capsize; and but for the blessings of the Lord in resuscitating Lorenzo Snow he would not have lived, because he was drowned upon that occasion. It was revealed to him, then and there, that the boy, with the courage of his convictions, with the iron will to be laughed at and scorned as lacking courage to get in that boat . . . would yet be the Prophet of God. Lorenzo Snow told me this upon more than one occasion, long years before Joseph F. Smith came to the presidency of the Church.[17]

Joseph F. Smith was ordained an Apostle on July 1, 1866, at age twenty-seven, by President Brigham Young; he was also ordained a counselor to the First Presidency on the same day. He was set apart as a member of the Quorum of the Twelve Apostles on October 8, 1867; released as a counselor to the First Presidency at the death of President Young on August 29, 1877; sustained as second counselor to President John Taylor on October 10, 1880; released at the death of President Taylor on July 25, 1887; sustained as second counselor to President Wilford Woodruff on April 7, 1889; sustained as second counselor to President Lorenzo Snow on September 13, 1898; sustained as first counselor to President Snow on October 6, 1901, not set apart to this position; released at the death of President Snow on October 10, 1901. Ordained and set apart as president of the Church on October 17, 1901, at age sixty-two. He passed away on November 19, 1918, at age eighty.[18]

Heber Jeddy Grant
Ordained Apostle on October 16, 1882

President Heber J. Grant, seventh president of the Church, related the following story:

> I was a child playing on the floor in a Relief Society meeting (my mother [Rachel Ridgeway Ivins] was president of the Thirteeth ward Relief Society . . .) when Eliza R. Snow blessed by the gift of tongues each of the presidents that happened to be in that meeting, and [my aunt] Zina D. Young gave the interpretation. After doing this she [Sister Snow] turned to the child (myself) playing upon the floor, and gave me a blessing, and Zina D. Young gave the interpretation.
>
> My mother often said to me, "Heber, behave yourself and you will some day be an Apostle."
>
> I laughed and told her I had no ambitions along that line. I said, "Get it out of your head. Every mother thinks that her son will be the President of the United States, or something wonderful. I do not want any Church position, I want to be a business man."
>
> "Never mind," she said, "if you behave yourself you will be an Apostle." When I was made an Apostle she asked me if I remembered that meeting. I told her I did.
>
> "'Do you remember anything that Sister Snow said?" I said: "No, I did not understand her." "Of course you did not, because she was speaking in an unknown tongue. Did you understand anything that Aunt Zina said?"
>
> "Only one thing, mother, I remember that as she was talking she lifted her hand and said that I would grow to be a big man, and since I have grown tall, I have often thought of that remark of hers." She said: "She did not say anything of the kind. She said you should grow to be a great man in The Church of Jesus Christ of Latter-day Saints, and become an Apostle of the Lord Jesus Christ."

She then said: "Do you remember being in a gathering in Brother Heber C. Kimball's home where there were a great many people, and after the dinner Brother Kimball picked you up and put you on the table and talked to you?" "Yes."

"Do you remember anything he said?" "Not a word. All I remember is I thought he had the blackest eyes I ever looked at, and I was frightened."

"Well, he prophesied that you should become one of the apostles of the Lord Jesus Christ, and live to be a greater man in the Church than your own father [Jedediah M. Grant, second counselor to President Brigham Young]; and that is the reason that I have told you that if you would behave yourself you would some day be an Apostle. I realized that if you did not behave yourself you never would attain to that position, no matter what you had been promised."[19]

Six years later, President Grant added this information:

My mother took me as a little baby to Patriarch William G. Perkins, who afterward located in St. George [Utah], and he gave me a short blessing, making a single page written in longhand, or a third of a typewritten page; but that little blessing foretells my whole life. I can testify that, by the inspiration of the living God, that man gave me that blessing. [Note these next words:] Years later, when as a young man not yet twenty-four years of age, I was called to be President of the Tooele [Utah] Stake, I had a [second] patriarchal blessing from the late John Rowberry, who, laying his hands upon my head, outlined my future life. He promised me in that blessing that I should be taken from Tooele county, and be made one of the leaders of Israel, and that I should become a leader of great magnitude among the people of God. That man laid his hands upon the head of Francis Marion Lyman, who was my predecessor as President of the Tooele Stake, and said to him: "Thy name shall be numbered among the Apostles of the Lord Jesus Christ in these latter days." Francis M. Lyman was taken from the Tooele Stake and made one of the Apostles of the Lord Jesus Christ in these latter days.[20]

Giving insightful information about the blessing given by Patriarch Rowberry, President Grant related the following:

> I know that He [God] inspired John Rowberry to give me a blessing that I should leave Tooele [Utah] and become one of the leading men in the Church, and it came true. And he said, "I saw something while blessing you that I dare not put in your blessing." [Note these words:] and it came to me as plain as though a voice had said it, "He saw you as the President of The Church of Jesus Christ of Latter-day Saints." I afterwards thought, "My gracious, I must be silly to think that that is true," and I never breathed it or said a word about it until that came to me. He gave me a marvelous blessing.[21]

Concerning his call to the apostleship, President Grant said:

> When the call came to me to be an apostle, the spirit of the adversary pursued me day and night, from October [16, 1882] until February [1883], telling me that I was unfit to occupy that exalted office. Every time that I bore witness of my knowledge that Jesus was the Christ, the words would fly back in my face: "You lie; you have not seen him." I would wake up in the night feeling that I should resign, that I was unworthy . . . I took a trip, in January, 1883, with [Elder] Brigham Young, Jr., to San Luis Valley, Colorado, to San Juan, to the Arizona Stakes, to Mexico, where we visited the Yaqui Indians . . .
>
> It was revealed to me there, sitting alone in the Navajo Indian Reservation, that I had done nothing to entitle me to the great honor of being an Apostle, except that I had kept my life pure and sweet. It was revealed to me there that a council was held in heaven, exactly the same as we hold councils here. Matters were discussed, and there was presented the question of filling the two vacancies existing in the quorum of the Twelve Apostles;

that the [General] conference had adjourned, and those two vacancies remained and ought to be filled. The question was: "Whom shall we call, in sending a revelation to fill those vacancies?" My father, Jedediah M. Grant [second Counselor to President Brigham Young], who died when I was a baby, only nine days old, asked God, our heavenly Father, that his son, Heber J. Grant, be called as an apostle, and Joseph Smith, the Prophet of this last dispensation . . . joined in the request made by my father, and the revelation was sent calling me to be an apostle of the Lord Jesus Christ.

No man, I believe, ever had less happiness or less joy than I had in proclaiming the gospel from October, 1882, when I was called to be an Apostle, until February, 1883, when the Lord Almighty gave to me this manifestation.[22]

HEBER J. GRANT AND GEORGE TEASDALE
EACH ORDAINED APOSTLE ON OCTOBER 16, 1882

As was mentioned by President Grant, two vacancies in the Quorum of the Twelve needed to be filled. The following gives insightful information on the men called to fill these vacancies:

"I was made one of the apostles in October, 1882. On the 6th of October, 1882, I met Brother George Teasdale at the south gate of the temple. His face lit up, and he said: 'Brother Grant, you and I—very enthusiastically—and then he commenced coughing and choking, and went on into meeting and did not finish his sentence. It came to me as plainly as though he had said the words: 'Are going to be chosen this afternoon to fill the vacancies in the Quorum of the Twelve Apostles.'

"I went to the meeting and my head swelled, and I thought to myself, 'Well, I am going to be one of the apostles,' and I was willing to vote for myself, but the conference adjourned without anyone being chosen."[23]

One can only imagine the thoughts that must have gone through the minds of Brother Grant and Brother Teasdale when each was not called to the apostleship at this general conference. President Grant recalls:

> Ten days later I received a telegram, . . . So I went to the President's office, and there sat Brother Teasdale, and all of the ten apostles, and the Presidency of Church

> [President John Taylor, George Q. Cannon, First Counselor, and Joseph F. Smith, Second Counselor] ... and the revelation was read calling Brother Teasdale and myself to the apostleship....
>
> After the meeting I said to Brother Teasdale, "I know what you were going to say to me on the sixth of October when you happened to choke half to death and then went into the meeting."
>
> He said, "Oh, no, you don't."
>
> "Yes, I do," and I repeated it: "You and I are going to be called to the apostleship."
>
> He said, "Well, that is what I was going to say, and then it occurred to me that I had no right to tell it, that I had received a manifestation from the Lord." He said, "Heber, I have suffered the tortures of the damned for ten days, thinking I could not tell the difference between a manifestation from the Lord and one from the devil, that the devil had deceived me."[24]

As to why Brothers Grant and Teasdale were not called to the apostleship at the October 1882 general conference, Elder Joseph Fielding Smith says, "This revelation [to President John Taylor] was given October 13, 1882, and the brethren were ordained three days later."[25]

In addition to the above, Elder Heber J. Grant wrote a letter to his cousin, Anthony W. Ivins, who would be ordained an apostle 25 years later:

> Well, Tony, your predictions made last March [1882] as we were going to St. George [Utah], that I would be one of the Apostles, has been fulfilled. You know the true sentiments of my heart on this subject, ... As advised in my last letter of the 16th, George Teasdale and myself were ordained as Apostles, the First Presidency and Twelve officiating. Brothers [Charles C.] Rich, [Albert] Carrington and [Moses] Thatcher [of the Twelve] were absent; President [John] Taylor was mouth in Brother Teasdale's ordination, President [George Q.] Cannon in mine.[26]

Later, in the letter President Grant wrote, "Dear Cousin, I feel with God's aid and the faith and prayers of my friends, especially those that know me as you do, that I shall be able to accomplish some good; without this assistance I shall fail in my calling as an Apostle. I can hardly realize that I am an Apostle. I suppose the fact will become more real as I get down to work."[27]

After he had become an Apostle, President Grant recorded the following:

> I thank the Lord that He saw fit to call me to be one of the Apostles.
>
> Shortly after my call to the apostleship I met Brother George Romney. He took hold of my hand, and the tears came in his eyes and he said, "Heber, the Lord gave to me a manifestation years ago when you were in your teens, when I was shaking hands with you. A voice said to me—and you did not hear it, but I did, as plain as could be—'An apostle of the Lord Jesus Christ of this last dispensation.' . . . I rejoice that that statement made to me has now been fulfilled by this revelation calling you."[28]

George Teasdale was ordained an Apostle on October 16, 1882, at age fifty, by President John Taylor. He passed away on June 9, 1907, at age seventy-five.[29]

Heber J. Grant was ordained an Apostle on October 16, 1882, at age twenty-five by George Q. Cannon; he became president of the Quorum of the Twelve Apostles on November 23, 1916; he was ordained and set apart as president of the Church on November 23, 1918, at age sixty-two. He passed away on May 14, 1945, at age eighty-eight.[30]

ABRAHAM HOAGLAND CANNON, ANTHON HENRIK LUND, AND MARRINER WOOD MERRILL
EACH ORDAINED AN APOSTLE ON OCTOBER 7, 1889

The following was related by President Wilford Woodruff, president of the Church on the day before each were sustained (October 6, 1889):

> I wish to say to this assemble of Latter-day Saints, that there are three vacancies in the Quorum of the Twelve Apostles, in consequence of the organization of the First Presidency. We have felt that it is the time to fill that Quorum now, at this Conference, and the people

should be prepared for the presenting by the Twelve Apostles of such names as they feel by the Spirit of God to be worthy and proper persons to receive this ordination or to occupy this position. These Apostles are Prophets, Seers and Revelators. I have confidence in them; I believe they have power to present such things as would be in accordance with the will of God. They (the apostles) presented to me a list of names. I wish here to say, and I want it understood, that neither myself, President George Q. Cannon nor President Joseph F. Smith, who are my Counselors, presented any of these names. We left it with the Quorum of the Apostles. I became thoroughly satisfied that they had upon that list such names as would be acceptable unto the Lord. We took those names and made it a matter of prayer, and the Spirit of the Lord manifested unto me those whom we should appoint. They have all been accepted by the Quorum of the Apostles as well as the Presidency of the Church.[31]

The names of Marriner W. Merrill, Anthon H. Lund, and Abraham H. Cannon were presented for sustaining vote. Elder Abraham H. Cannon wrote of his call to the Apostleship, saying:

> At 9:00 a.m. I went to the Gardo House where myself and Bro. Anthon H. Lund of Ephraim, Sanpete Co., were summoned into the presence of the First Presidency and Twelve Apostles. Pres. Woodruff then stated that Bro. Marriner W. Merrill and ourselves had been selected to fill the vacancies in the Quorum of the Twelve. . . . The names of Bros. Marriner W. Merrill, Anthon H. Lund, and Abraham H. Cannon were then presented separately, and the vote on each was unanimous.[32]

Concerning their ordination to the apostleship, Elder Cannon wrote:

> At 3 p.m. I attended a meeting of the Twelve at the Gardo House when Bros. Merrill, Lund, and myself were set apart as Apostles in the order named. President Woodruff set apart the first, [who was Marriner W.

> Merrill] [my] Father [George Q. Cannon set apart] the second [who was Anthon H. Lund] and Bro. Joseph F. [Smith set apart] myself. Our charge was first given us by [my] Father at Pres. W[oodruff]'s [request]. The importance of our callings was portrayed, and our privileges were named. Among these were the privileges of having the ministration of angels, and of seeing the Savior Himself, of hearing the voice of God as audibly as we hear a man's voice, of continually being under the direction of the Holy Ghost, of being prophets and revelators; and of many other things of which I have a verbatim copy, as also of my blessing and ordination, in which I was promised everything my heart desired in righteousness if faithful.[33]

Marriner W. Merrill was ordained an Apostle on October 7, 1889, at age fifty-seven, by President Wilford Woodruff. He passed away on February 6, 1906, at age seventy-three.

Anthon H. Lund was ordained an Apostle on October 7, 1889, at age forty-five, by George Q. Cannon. He was sustained as second counselor to President Joseph F. Smith on October 17, 1901; sustained as first counselor to President Smith on April 7, 1910; and sustained as first counselor to President Heber J. Grant on November 23, 1918. He passed away on March 2, 1921, at age seventy-six.

Abraham H. Cannon was ordained an Apostle on October 7, 1889, at age thirty by Joseph F. Smith. He passed away on July 19, 1896, at age thirty-seven.[34]

MATTHIAS FOSS COWLEY
ORDAINED APOSTLE ON OCTOBER 7, 1897

Elder Matthias F. Cowley is the father of Elder Matthew Cowley of the Twelve. Matthias F. Cowley shares the following regarding his calling:

> On the 5th day of July, 1876, I was told by the Patriarch Wm. McBride, "Thou must prepare thy mind, for the time is not far distant when thou shalt be called into the ministry, and shalt travel much for the Gospel's sake both at home and abroad." From my earliest remembrances I had anticipated that at some future time, I

would, like other young men, be called to "fill a mission," but from the time the Patriarch uttered the words quoted above upon my head, the spirit of studying the scriptures and preparing my heart for the work, rested upon me more intensely than ever before. Accordingly I studied and memorized many passages of Scripture upon the fundamental principles of the Gospel, which proved to be of inestimable value to me in subsequent years.[35]

In addition to this patriarchal blessing, Brother Cowley received a letter, part of which included this:

> While laboring in Rochester, Butler County, Kentucky, March 19, 1882 . . . he [John W. Taylor, son of President John Taylor, who was ordained an Apostle by his father on April 9, 1884] wrote a letter to Elder Matthias F. Cowley, who at the time was also [Note: both were serving a mission for the Church] laboring as a missionary in St. Louis, Missouri. In this letter he made this prediction: "I believe I speak by the spirit of prophecy when I say, if you are faithful you will yet become one of the Twelve Apostles of the Church of Jesus Christ in all the world, and by the power of God and the eternal Priesthood will become great in wisdom and knowledge. Amen." No one but the two Elders knew of this prophecy until after its fulfillment, fifteen years later, when Elder Cowley was chosen and ordained an Apostle.[36]

The following is written in *Essentials in Church History*:

> "While the investigation [of Reed Smoot of the Twelve to become a United States Senator from Utah] at Washington [D. C.] was going on, Elders John W. Taylor and Matthias F. Cowley were requested by the senate committee as witnesses. President [Joseph F.] Smith was asked to locate them and have them go to Washington. In answer to his appeal they declined to go. It was discovered that they were out of harmony with the attitude of the Church regarding the manifesto of President [Wilford] Woodruff. They maintained that the manifesto applied to the United

States only. However, the attitude of the Church was that it applied to the entire world.[37]

Later, the "agitation which followed led to the resignation, October 28, 1905, of Elders John W. Taylor and Matthias F. Cowley from the council of the Apostles."[38]

Providing another point of view, Elder Spencer W. Kimball wrote, "In 1906, my father received a letter from his dear friend, Matthias F. Cowley, who had been greatly embarrassed by being dropped from the Council of the Twelve. His letter showed great courage and a sweet, unembittered spirit: 'In relation to the trial which has come to me, I will say that I accept it in all humility and meekness, with no fault to find against my brethren, but a strong desire to continue faithful and to devote my life and all my energies in the service of the Lord.'"[39]

Matthias F. Cowley was ordained an Apostle on October 7, 1897, at age thirty-nine, by George Q. Cannon. He resigned on October 28, 1905; his priesthood was suspended on May 11, 1911; he was restored to full membership on April 3, 1936. He passed away on June 16, 1940, at age eighty-one.[40]

RUDGER CLAWSON
ORDAINED APOSTLE ON OCTOBER 10, 1898

Elder Rudger Clawson wrote this about his life as a member of the Twelve:

> My life as an apostle is very similar to the life of all the other eleven apostles. I do not know that there is any radical difference. Our experiences are very much the same, so that if I speak of my experience briefly, you will know that it is the experience of all of the apostles. I doubt whether there is an apostle in the Church today that can give information about himself, such as I will give you concerning myself. I doubt if there is an apostle that keeps such a careful record as I do. I will tell you what my record is, and in a general way how I keep it.
>
> I have what is called a skeleton journal. It is not one of those horrifying skeletons, but it is a skeleton of a journal, in which all of the drudgery and unimportant things are cut out, and just the salient facts retained.[41]

In another part of his memoirs, Elder Clawson tells of his call to the Apostleship:

> My tenure of office as President of the Box Elder Stake of Zion covered a period of practically eleven years, viz., from January 1888 to October 1898.
>
> At one of the sessions of the semi-annual General Conference of the Church held in the Salt Lake City Tabernacle in October, 1898, the General Authorities of the Church were presented and sustained by the unanimous vote of the conference. At this time it was announced by President George Q. Cannon that a vacancy had been created in the Quorum of the Twelve Apostles by the removal of President Snow from it to assume the position of President of the Church, that it had been decided to fill this vacancy and that the mind and will of the Lord had been obtained upon the selection of Rudger Clawson for this office. A motion was made and put to the several quorums and to the entire congregation that I be ordained an apostle and made a member of the Council of the Twelve. The voting was unanimously affirmative.
>
> Thus without previous intimation I became a member of that important council of men which is next in authority to the First Presidency of the Church. It may well be imagined that I felt weak and humble in view of the tremendous responsibility that had thus suddenly fallen upon me....
>
> This call that has come has proven to be a very great surprise. I had no knowledge of it; I had no notice of it whatever, only as it has come to me today in this meeting [right after the call]. [Note these next words:] My patriarchal blessing that was given in 1883 indicated that I would be called to a high appointment in the Church in the due time of the Lord. I presume that this is the appointment....
>
> On October 10, 1898, at a meeting in the Temple, I was ordained an apostle in the Council of the Twelve apostles under the hands of the following brethren:

Lorenzo Snow, George Q. Cannon, Joseph F. Smith, Franklin D. Richards, Brigham Young, Jr., Francis M. Lyman, John Henry Smith, George Teasdale, Heber J. Grant, John W. Taylor, Marriner W. Merrill, Anthon H. Lund, Matthias F. Cowley and Abraham O. Woodruff. With President Snow officiating, the ordination was as follows:

"Brother Rudger Clawson, in the name of the Lord Jesus and by virtue of the holy priesthood, we place our hands upon your head and we ordain you an apostle in the Quorum of the Twelve Apostles, and we confer upon you all the gifts, blessings, rights, keys and powers that pertain unto this holy and sacred apostleship. And we say unto you, Brother Rudger, in the name of the Lord, inasmuch as you will be humble and seek the Lord for His Spirit, it shall be given as the spirit of revelation upon you, which it is your privilege to have as an apostle, and to testify of your own knowledge that there is a God over the inhabitants of the earth, and that there is a Jesus, the Son of the living God, who was crucified upon Mount Calvary—that you may testify of this, having a most perfect knowledge of it by the power of God and the Holy Ghost. All the blessings, all the qualifications, and all that is necessary to make you perfect in this apostleship, in the name of the Lord Jesus we seal upon you, and say that these blessings that we have sealed upon you shall continue upon you during your life, and also throughout all eternity. These blessings, gifts, powers, rights and keys we seal upon you in the name of the Lord Jesus, Amen."

President Lorenzo Snow delivered the following charge to me:

"A few words I want to say as to the obligation you are placed under now that you have received the apostleship. The Lord will reveal unto you, according to your faithfulness and the circumstances, the duties that will be required of you. You must understand that it is not man that has chosen you; it is not the wisdom of man that has selected you. . . . But you have been chosen because the Lord wanted you to fill this place and because of your faithfulness in the past. . . .

"You are now, of course, the youngest of the apostles, so far as coming into the quorum is concerned. There are many in this quorum who have been in this relation to the Church as apostles for a great many years, and have had a long experience, and the Lord has blessed them wonderfully. You must not expect that at once you can feel yourself at home and be equal with them in that knowledge which they have obtained through perseverance and a long movement in the path of duty. . . . You will, of course, not feel it your duty to take up all the time, but to let others speak. Let those who have had long experience speak when it comes to matters of high importance, and you listen. Do not occupy too much time at first. Wait until you have had the experience and get the wisdom and understanding the Lord has given to them and will give to you."[42]

"President Joseph F. Smith said: . . . 'I thought I would like to mention this fact that one of the great callings and special duties of the apostles is to become a living witness of the Lord Jesus Christ, to know him, and to be able to testify that He is the Son of God and the Savior of the world. That is essential to the calling of an apostle of Jesus Christ.' . . .

"President George Q. Cannon added: 'I would like Brother Rudger Clawson to understand when he takes upon himself this ministry that it is the first and most important thing; that he should not set this aside to attend to anything else. His whole life and all that pertains to his power of life, his talents and everything should be exclusively to the apostleship, and everything else should be entirely subordinate to that."

I responded as follows: "All that I can say, brethren, is that I very much appreciate the instructions and the suggestions that have been given, and I fully and completely accept and endorse them. I feel very weak, a great deal more so than I did at Conference. Since then I have come to think the matter over, and a great deal has opened up to my mind. If I could not feel that this call has come to me from the Lord, I should shrink from it, I could not accept it, because the responsibility of it, it seems to me, is so very great that no man of his own wisdom could magnify a calling of this kind. . . . I pray fervently that the spirit of this appointment and the spirit of the apostleship may rest upon me . . . in the name of Jesus Christ. Amen."

I was soon to learn that the members of the Council of the Twelve of necessity lead an exceedingly active and strenuous life.[43]

Rudger Clawson was ordained an Apostle on October 10, 1898, at age forty-one, by President Lorenzo Snow. He was sustained as second counselor to President Snow on October 6, 1901; released at the death of President Snow on October 10, 1901; resumed his position in the Quorum of the Twelve Apostles; and sustained as president of the Quorum of the Twelve Apostles on March 17, 1921. He passed away on June 21, 1943, at age eighty-six.[44]

GEORGE ALBERT SMITH
ORDAINED APOSTLE ON OCTOBER 8, 1903

As has been mentioned, President George Albert Smith, the eighth president of the Church, is the son of Elder John Henry Smith of the Twelve. He too received a heads-up regarding his call in a blessing:

A patriarchal blessing was once again the device used by the Lord in warning George Albert Smith. President Smith was only fourteen years of age when the patriarch placed his hands upon the young man's head and pronounced this blessing:

"Thou shalt become a mighty prophet in the midst of the sons of Zion. And the angels of the Lord shall administer unto you, and the choice blessing of the heavens shall rest upon you. . . . And thou shalt be wrapt in the visions of the heavens and thou shalt be clothed with salvation as with a garment, for thou are destined to become a mighty man before the Lord, for thou shalt become a mighty Apostle in the Church and kingdom of God upon the earth for none of thy father's family shall have more power with God than thou shalt have, for none shall exceed thee . . . and thou shalt become a man of mighty faith before the Lord, even like unto that of the brother of Jared, and thou shall remain upon the earth until thou art satisfied with life, and shall be numbered with the Lord's anointed and shall become a king and a priest unto the Most High."[45]

Elder John Henry Smith, father of Elder George Albert Smith, wrote the following in his diary:

Sunday, October 4, 1903
Salt Lake City, Utah

President Jos. F. Smith said to me tonight that the mind of the Spirit was that my son George Albert should fill the vacancy in the Apostles. I told him was it a political office I would advise against it but I could not stand in the way of the suggestion of the Spirit to him.

Tuesday, October 6, 1903
Salt Lake City, Utah

All of the First Presidency and Patriarch and of the Apostles, myself, George Teasdale, Heber J. Grant, John W. Taylor, Matthias F. Cowley, Abraham O. Woodruff, Rudger Clawson, Reed Smoot, and Hyrum Smith met in council in the President's office.

Prayer by John R. Winder

President Joseph F. Smith said the mind of the Spirit to him was that George A[lbert] Smith fill the vacancy in the Council of the Apostles. It was sustained unanimously—all speaking their minds.

Benediction by A. H. Lund.[46]

Elder George Albert Smith shared the following in a general conference:

I attended the general conferences that were held semi-annually in this building [Salt Lake Tabernacle]. I used to edge my way in and sit down on the stairs at the left. The house would be full, and there weren't seats for everybody. On the particular occasion to which I refer [October 4, 1903], I came in, as usual, and worked my way through the crowd and finally got a seat down near the bottom of the stairs. . . . Presiding Bishop Charles W. Nibley, who was my neighbor, touched me on the shoulder and said, "Come and sit by me." I said, "'There is plenty of room here." Again he said, "Come and sit by me. It is more comfortable here." If I had known what was going to happen during that conference, you could not have pried me into that seat.

That was on Sunday [October 4, 1903]. I had to be at my work in the land office because people were there from all over, and I could not go to the meetings except on Sunday. The following Tuesday [October 6, 1903], I came home from the land office to take my children down to the fair at four o'clock, and Sister Nellie Colebrook Taylor came across the street and said, "Oh, Brother Smith, I congratulate you."

I said, "What are you congratulating me about?"

She said, "Don't you know?"

I replied, "I don't know what you are talking about."

"Why," she said, "you have just been sustained as a member of the Quorum of the Twelve." And I talked her out of it.

She apologized and said, "I am sorry. I hope you will forgive me." Knowing what my father's experiences had been, and having such a nice position at the land office, I was not looking for a place such as father [John Henry Smith, of the Twelve] had. It took all his time and kept him away from home so much.

I turned to my wife and said, "I will take the children now and go down to the fair." But before I could get to the buggy, back came Sister Taylor, and she rushed up to me and said, "It was you! It was you! Everybody heard it."

I will never forget how I felt. I turned to my wife, and she was in tears. That is the way I received my notice that I had been sustained as a member of the Quorum of the Twelve.[47]

George Albert Smith was ordained an Apostle on October 8, 1903, at age thirty-three, by President Joseph F. Smith; sustained as president of the Quorum of the Twelve Apostles on July 1, 1943. He was ordained and set apart as president of the Church on May 21, 1945, at age seventy-five; he passed away on April 4, 1951, at age eight-one.[48]

CHARLES WILLIAM PENROSE
ORDAINED APOSTLE ON JULY 7, 1904

President Charles W. Penrose of the First Presidency related the following:

> [Orson Pratt and I] traveled together, I remember very well, at one time through Cache Valley and in different settlements we had the opportunity of sharing each other's feelings and sentiments, and I have always felt thankful in my soul that I had his confidence, and was honored with his goodwill, and I may say in passing that he foreshadowed my connection with the quorum of the Twelve Apostles. I don't know that I have ever mentioned that before, but he foretold that I would be numbered with the Apostles.[49]

Charles W. Penrose was ordained an Apostle on July 7, 1904, at age seventy-two, by President Joseph F. Smith. He was sustained as second counselor to President Smith on December 7, 1911; sustained as second counselor to President Heber J. Grant on November 23, 1918; and sustained as first counselor to President Grant on March 10, 1921. He passed away on May 15, 1925, at age ninety-three.[50]

ORSON FERGUSON WHITNEY
ORDAINED APOSTLE ON APRIL 9, 1906

Elder Orson F. Whitney wrote the following, noting, "It was March, 1886, when Lorenzo Snow [of the Twelve] was sent to the Utah Penitentiary, convicted upon three separate indictments for one offense, and sentenced by Associate Justice Orlando W. Powers to the aggregate term of eighteen months imprisonment."[51]

Concerning these indictments, Elder Joseph Fielding Smith wrote, "During the anti-polygamy crusade, he [Elder Snow] was sentenced . . . under the 'segregation' ruling, to serve three terms of imprisonment of six months each, making a period of eighteen months, and to pay three fines of three hundred dollars each."⁵²

Returning to Elder Whitney's words, we read:

> On July 4th, at the close of the prison service, at which I was the speaker, I had an interview with the venerable Apostle, and in the course of it predicted that he would not serve out his full term. "Well, I came prepared for it," said he resignedly. I then repeated the prediction.
>
> He had spent eleven of the eighteen months behind bolts and bars, when a decision from the Supreme Court of the United States shattered the illegal doctrine of "segregation" under which he had been convicted, and he went forth a free man. Meeting him at the [Salt Lake] Tabernacle shortly afterwards, I said: "I told you, you wouldn't serve out your full [prison] term." "That's so, you did," was his smiling answer, "You are a prophet—you are a prophet."
>
> That little incident was the beginning of a close friendship between Brother Snow and myself. I spent many happy hours in his society, mainly at his home in Brigham City [Utah]. We interchanged confidences, and he employed my pen in the production of a biographical sketch covering the period of his [polygamy "segregation"] trial and imprisonment. While setting me apart for this task, he prophesied that I would "be lifted up and occupy places high and glorious in this life."⁵³

In conjunction with this prophesy, we read these informative words:

> At the town of Hyrum [Utah], I became acquainted with . . . O. N. Liljenquist, the bishop of that ward, who was also a patriarch. From him I received my first patriarchal blessing, and it was a great comfort to me. I had been very downhearted over the unpromising state of my [physical] health, and the patriarch's words, fraught with the spirit of his holy calling, lifted me from . . . despondency. He told me that while his hands were on my head my life passed before him like a panorama. He predicted

to certain friends of mine, and subsequently to me, that I would yet be an Apostle. The date of the repeated prediction was April 6, 1886, twenty years before I was called to the Apostleship. Whenever I met this good man he had something to say about my future. "You will go upon many missions," said he, "and will pass through some narrow places, but will come out just about as successfully as a man ever did."[54]

In addition to Elder Lorenzo Snow's prophesy, Elder Whitney mentions another one:

"During January and July, 1887, I preached in all the principal wards of Bear Lake Stake and in many of the towns of Central and Southern Utah, both trips being planned by Elder John W. Taylor, of the Council of the Twelve, who invited me to accompany him. . . . In the south, Brother Taylor and I, with my son Race, went as far as Woolley's Ranch near Kanab [Utah]—my first visit to that section.

Not long afterward, while the Apostle and I were traveling together, he prophesied that I would yet be one of the Twelve. He little knew, nor did I, that my call and ordination to the Apostleship, twenty years later, would fill a vacancy caused by his own retirement. [Meaning: When he and Elder Matthias F. Cowley were out of harmony with the attitude of the Church regarding the manifesto of President Wilford Woodruff.][55]

Orson F. Whitney was ordained an Apostle on April 9, 1906, at age fifty, by President Joseph F. Smith. He passed away on May 16, 1931, at age seventy-five.[56]

DAVID OMAN MCKAY
ORDAINED APOSTLE ON APRIL 9, 1906

President David O. McKay was the ninth president of the Church. The younger David O. McKay was just finishing his mission—the European Mission—when a special Scottish Conference was held on May 29, 1899. The mission presidency consisted of Platte D. Lyman, president; James L. McMurrin, first counselor; and Henry W. Naisbitt, second counselor. With this information, we turn to the expressions of President McKay:

> I had learned by intimate association . . . that James McMurrin was pure gold. His faith in the gospel was implicit. No truer man, no man more loyal to what he thought was right ever lived. So when he turned to me and gave what I thought then was more of a caution than a promise, his words made an indelible impression upon me. Paraphrasing the words of the Savior to Peter, Brother McMurrin said: "Let me say to you, Brother David, Satan hath desired you that he may sift you as wheat, but God is mindful of you." Then he added, "If you will keep the faith, you will yet sit in the leading councils of the Church."[57]

David O. McKay was ordained an Apostle on April 9, 1906, at age thirty-two, by President Joseph F. Smith. He was sustained as second counselor to President Heber J. Grant on October 6, 1934; sustained as second counselor to President George Albert Smith on May 21, 1945; sustained as president of the Quorum of the Twelve Apostles on September 30, 1950; sustained as president of the Church on April 9, 1951, at age seventy-seven. He passed away on January 18, 1970, at age ninety-six.[58]

ANTHONY WOODWARD IVINS
ORDAINED APOSTLE ON OCTOBER 6, 1907

Elder Anthony W. Ivins is the cousin of President Heber J. Grant, seventh president of the Church. In his personal journal, he wrote,

"I slept at Bro. Henry Luntz last night in the same bed with Apostle [Francis M.] Lyman. I dreamed that I was at a meeting where Apostle Lyman was talking and that in the course of his remarks he said that I had been called by the Lord to preside over the Mexican Mission and that I would in the future be called to the Apostleship."[59]

Concerning Brother Ivins's call to be president of the stake in Mexico, President Grant related the following:

> I thank God for a testimony that came to me, the external part of me, the day Brother Ivins was called to Mexico. Brother George Q. Cannon [Counselor in the First Presidency] made the remark, "I do not want Brother

Ivins to go to Mexico, we need him here. He is the outstanding man in his party in Utah, but I believe the Lord wants him there." When he was called I felt a little sad, and while thinking about it, the Lord saw fit to give me this word: "You need not feel bad, he is going where the Lord wants him to go and you shall have the exquisite joy of welcoming him back into this room as one of the Apostles of the Lord Jesus Christ." I was in the Apostles' room in the temple at the time. I turned my head and wept for joy."[60]

To illustrate that the Lord inspires faithful members of the Church to know who will be called to the leading councils of the Church, we read the following by President Grant to Brother Ivins:

I think that I told you that [my] mother informed your mother in my presence that she knew that some day that you would be an Apostle. Your mother insisted that she made this remark because of her great love for you, but mother was very positive that she had this knowledge by the inspiration of the Lord. I am grateful to know that she was so inspired . . .

Your affectionate cousin, HEBER J. GRANT.[61]

Elder Ivins wrote about his name being presented as a member of the Twelve Apostles:

As I wrote the exercises of the [General] Conference yesterday, I wrote the names of the Presidency as they were presented by Pres. Smith. He then presented the name of F. M. Lyman as President of the Quorum of Apostles, and then to fill the vacancy caused by the death of Geo. Teasdale presented my name. I was so overcome that I could not write. Immediately after Conference adjourned I went with the Presidency and Quorum of Apostles to the President's Office and after instructing me in regard to my duties as a member of the Quorum, the Presidency and Twelve laid their hands on me and Pres. Smith ordained me a member of the Quourm.[62]

Anthony W. Ivins was ordained an Apostle on October 6, 1907, at age fifty-five, by President Joseph F. Smith. He was sustained as second counselor to President Heber J. Grant on March 10, 1921 and sustained as first counselor to President Grant on May 28, 1925. He passed away on September 23, 1934, at age eighty-two.[64]

Joseph Fielding Smith
ORDAINED APOSTLE ON APRIL 7, 1910

As has been mentioned, President Joseph Fielding Smith, tenth president of the Church, is the brother of Elder Hyrum Mack Smith, of the Twelve, and the son of President Joseph F. Smith, sixth president of the Church. D. Arthur Haycock, who was the secretary to five Church Presidents, wrote about President Smith:

> Seventy-six years ago at the age of twenty, President [Joseph Fielding] Smith received his patriarchal blessing, a portion of which I should like to read to you.
>
> "It is thy privilege to live to a good old age and the will of the Lord that you should become a mighty man in Israel. Thou shalt realize that thy life has been preserved for a wise purpose.
>
> "Thou hast much to do in order to complete thy mission upon the earth. It shall be thy duty to sit in council with thy brethren and to preside among the people. Hold up thy head; lift up thy voice without fear or favor as the Spirit of the Lord shall direct. His spirit shall direct thy mind and give thee word and sentiment that thou shalt confound the wisdom of the wicked men and set at naught the councils of the unjust."
>
> I think you and I can all attest that this blessing given three quarters of a century ago has been and is being literally fulfilled in the life of this wonderful man. He is a good man, a great man, kind and gentle and humble, a servant of the Lord, the prophet of the Lord.[64]

Elder Bruce R. McConkie, a son-in-law of President Joseph Fielding Smith, said this:

> President Smith was born as a child of promise. Asked recently in my presence how he got his name, he

said, "I came by it honestly." The fact is that his father, President Joseph F. Smith, had three of his five wives at the time, and had promised Julina Lambson that her first son would be named Joseph Fielding, Jr.

Julina had three daughters but no sons, and so she went before the Lord, and like Hannah of Old, "vowed a vow." Her promise: that if the Lord would give her a son, "she would do all in her power to help him be a credit to the Lord and to his father." The Lord hearkened to her prayers, and she kept her promise to him; and he also manifested to her, before the birth of the man child, that her son would be called to serve in the Council of the Twelve. . . .

When President Smith was 20 years of age, he received a patriarchal blessing from John Smith, the Patriarch to the Church. This inspired man told him, in the Lord's name, that he would "live to a good old age" and become "a mighty man in Israel."

"It shall be thy duty," inspired declaration announced, "to sit in council with thy brethren and to preside among the people. It shall be thy duty also to travel much, at home and abroad by land and water, laboring in the ministry; and I say unto thee: Hold up thy head; lift up thy voice without fear or favor as the Spirit of the Lord shall direct; and the blessing of the Lord shall rest upon thee. His Spirit shall direct they mind and give thee word and sentiment that thou shalt confound the wisdom of the wicked and set at naught the councils of the unjust."

If ever the promises of a patriarch found complete fulfillment, such was the case with these inspired utterances.[65]

Concerning his call to serve as a member of the Quorum of the Twelve Apostles, we read:

As Joseph Fielding Smith walked through the gate of the Salt Lake Temple grounds to attend the concluding session of the April Conference in 1910, one of the gatekeepers asked him, "Well, who is going to be called to fill the vacancy in the Council of the Twelve today?" Joseph Fielding replied, "I don't know, but there is one thing I do know—it won't be me and it won't be you." He continued on into the meeting and took his seat.

His father [President Joseph F. Smith] called the meeting to order and announced the opening hymn, 'We Thank Thee, Oh God, For A Prophet.' The invocation was offered by [Elder] Brigham H. Roberts, following which the [Tabernacle] Choir sang the hymn, 'The Spirit of God Like A Fire Is Burning.' Then [Elder] Heber J. Grant arose to present the names of the General Authorities for a sustaining vote. About thirty seconds before he got to the point where he would read the name of the new apostle, Joseph Fielding suddenly knew that the name that would be read was his. (In those days it was not the common practice to talk to the person concerned in advance.) He was right.[66]

Elder Joseph Anderson, assistant to the Twelve, wrote this:

As I think back, I recall that many years ago Sister Noah S. Pond, who was a relative of Joseph Fielding Smith, told me that on one occasion when she was a young girl and was at a party where Brother Smith was also present, a voice very distinctly told her that someday that young man would be the president of the Church. I recall that when she related this to me, I also had the burning assurance in my own soul that this would be the case. As I associated over the years with President Smith, learned to know the purity of his heart, heard his burning testimony, and felt the majesty of his soul, this assurance not only remained but grew stronger and stronger. I was certain that he was destined to become our prophet and president. I must confess, however, that when he became 92 years of age and then 93, I wondered if I was mistaken.[67]

Joseph Fielding Smith was ordained an Apostle on April 7, 1910, at age thirty-three, by President Joseph F. Smith. He was sustained as acting president of the Quorum of the Twelve Apostles on September

30, 1950; sustained as president of the Quorum of the Twelve Apostles on April 9, 1951; and sustained as a counselor in the First Presidency on October 29, 1965. He was ordained and set apart as president of the Church on January 23, 1970, at age ninety-three; he passed away on July 2, 1972, at age ninety-five.[68]

MELVIN JOSEPH BALLARD
ORDAINED APOSTLE ON JANUARY 7, 1919

Elder Melvin J. Ballard is the grandfather of Elder M. Russell Ballard of the Twelve. President Heber J. Grant related the following:

> I have been happy during the twenty-two years that it has fallen my lot to stand at the head of this Church. I have felt the inspiration of the Living God directing me in my labors. From the day that I chose a comparative stranger to be one of the Apostles, instead of my lifelong and dearest living friend, I have known as I know that I live, that I am entitled to the light and the inspiration and the guidance of God in directing His work here upon this earth.[69]

Providing additional information about the calling of this "comparative stranger," Elder Spencer W. Kimball wrote:

> During the years he was a member of the Council of the Twelve, President Heber J. Grant often recommended names of brethren to the First Presidency for consideration as apostles. Frequently he thought that if he ever were President of the Church he would appoint his lifelong friend. . . . Richard W. Young, a grandson of President Brigham Young, to the apostleship. However, when he did become President he chose instead, under the inspiration of the Lord, a relative stranger to him, Elder Melvin J. Ballard.[70]

Melvin J. Ballard was ordained an Apostle on January 7, 1919, at age forty-five, by President Heber J. Grant. He passed away on July 30, 1939, at age sixty-six.[71]

Alonzo Arza Hinckley
ORDAINED APOSTLE ON OCTOBER 11, 1934

Elder Alonzo Hinckley, uncle of President Gordon B. Hinckley, received a unique blessing. Here's the story of that blessing:

> Millard Stake had just closed its quarterly conference. It was the first one since the new president, Alonzo A. Hinckley had been installed. That was back in 1903, thirty-four years ago, and the new officer was succeeding his father [Ira N. Hinckley]. He was in his thirty-third year. . . .
>
> It happened also that, in Millard Stake, there lived a man named John Ashman. John Ashman . . . usually taught one of the classes in the lesser priesthood. . . . Another of his religious duties was to give patriarchal blessings. Usually people came to him for this purpose, but sometimes he went to them. . . .
>
> At this particular quarterly conference Patriarch Ashman was present. He was more than present. For, while President Hinckley was officiating in his new calling, Brother Ashman's patriarchal spirit manifested itself. He saw more than met the eye. After the close of the meeting the Patriarch asked the President if he would not stay for a few minutes. "I want to give you a blessing," he explained. Although Brother Hinckley thought the request somewhat odd, and although he was in a hurry to get home, yet he consented to stay. . . . President Hinckley, Patriarch Ashman, and George A. Seaman, one of the counselors in the Stake Presidency, retired to a room by themselves, where they would not be disturbed. And under these circumstances a blessing was given to the new president.
>
> The blessing was even more extraordinary than the request. Said the patriarch, among other things: "If you continue to labor with the zeal you have started in with, you will be numbered with the Twelve Apostles of The Church of Jesus Christ of Latter-day Saints."
>
> That, remember, was back in 1903. Time passed. . . . Meantime, he [President Alonzo A. Hinckley] paid no

particular attention to the blessing. As a matter of fact, he was inclined to believe it to have originated in a strong desire on the part of the Patriarch, rather than dictated by the Spirit. Patriarch Ashman had taught him for many years in the Aaronic Priesthood, he had liked him and praised him as one of the good boys in the ward, and it was only natural that his teacher should desire a blessing for him of a signal character. Indeed, at the time the blessing was given President Hinckley requested the Patriarch to say nothing about the matter to any one. President Hinckley himself never mentioned it to even his wife or any member of his family.

In the year 1934, thirty-one years after the blessing, Elder Hinckley was called to be one of the Twelve Apostles.

Says Brother Seaman, who took down the blessing: "I acted as scribe, and felt the inspiration that prompted the words of the blessing. I have waited patiently for their fulfillment, knowing that you (Elder Hinckley) have unceasingly followed the admonition therein given, and by your labors merited those blessings, and even greater ones." This was said in a letter to Elder Hinckley after he was made an Apostle.

After his call to the Apostleship Elder Hinckley said to one of his sons, "I feel as if I would like to go down on my knees to Brother Ashman and ask his forgiveness for doubting, even for a moment, his inspiration as he gave me that blessing."[72]

In conjunction with this special blessing, President Joseph Fielding Smith, president of the Twelve Apostles, said:

> I know of one or two cases of that where a brother has been blessed by the patriarch and told that he would become a member of the Council of the Twelve. Usually a patriarch doesn't say that, even if he feels that the chances are that a man will be called to the leading councils of the Church.

> I want to tell you of this one story of Alonzo A. Hinckley, and some of you will remember Alonzo A. Hinckley, who presided in the Deseret Stake for a number of years. He received a blessing, and in that blessing the patriarch said that the time would come when he would be ordained and placed in the Council of the Twelve. Brother Hinckley said to himself, "That's an impossibility." He took his blessing and put it away and said, "I became disappointed: I knew it couldn't be fulfilled: I lost my faith in the patriarch, and my blessing did not serve me as it should have done." Well Alonzo A. Hinckley was called into the Council of the Twelve.
>
> In giving their blessings patriarchs should be very careful to not make extravagant expressions and to be conservative in what they say; but if the Lord does speak to them and tell them to say something, they have the inspiration and it's their right to say it."[73]

Alonzo A. Hinckley was ordained an Apostle on October 11, 1934, at age sixty-four, by President Heber J. Grant. He passed away on December 22, 1936, at age sixty-six.[74]

SPENCER WOOLLEY KIMBALL
ORDAINED APOSTLE ON OCTOBER 7, 1943

President Spencer W. Kimball, twelfth president of the Church, is a grandson of President Heber C. Kimball, first counselor to President Brigham Young. Elder Mark E. Petersen of the Twelve wrote about President Kimball, saying: "While yet a boy, he [Spencer W. Kimball] was spoken of by his father in prophecy. Andrew Kimball, president of the St. Joseph Stake in Arizona, under the power of the Holy Ghost, spoke of his son's willingness to obey and then said: 'I have dedicated him to be one of the mouthpieces of the Lord. You will see him some day as a great leader. I have dedicated him to the service of God and he will become a mighty man in the Church.'"[75]

Dr. Russell M. Nelson, renowned heart surgeon, who was ordained an Apostle twelve years later, shares his comments:

> President Kimball [then Acting President of the Quorum of the Twelve Apostles] attended only one of

the seven sessions of general conference in April 1972. His breathlessness and inability to exert himself because of his congestive heart failure forced him to listen to the other sessions from his bed.

On the eve of the operation, April 11, 1972, I received a blessing, at my request, from the First Presidency under the hands of President Harold B. Lee and President Nathan Eldon Tanner. They blessed me that the operation would be performed without error, that all would go well, and that I need not fear for my own inadequacies, for I had been raised up by the Lord to perform this operation.

On April 12, 1972, the operation was performed. As the skin incision was made, my resident exclaimed, "He doesn't bleed!" From that very first maneuver until the last one, everything went as planned. There was not one broken stitch, not one instrument had fallen from the table, not one technical flaw had occurred in a series of thousands of intricate manipulations . . . a long and difficult operation had been performed exactly in accordance with the blessing invoked by the power of the priesthood.

But even more special than that was the overpowering feeling that came upon me as we shocked his heart, and it resumed its beating immediately with power and vigor. The Spirit told me that I had just operated upon a man who would become president of the Church!

I knew that President Kimball was a prophet. I knew that he was an apostle, but now it was revealed to me that he would preside over the Church! This feeling was so strong that I could hardly contain myself as we performed the routine maneuvers to conclude the operation. Later on in the week as he convalesced, I shared this news with him, and he and I both wept. I know that he did not take this feeling as seriously as I did because he knew that President Harold B. Lee, who stood before him in the Quorum, was younger and more healthy than he. Nonetheless, he honored my expression of the feelings as I had accurately and honestly reported them to him.[76]

Spencer W. Kimball was ordained an Apostle on October 7, 1943, at age forty-eight, by President Heber J. Grant. He was set apart as acting president of the Quorum of the Twelve Apostles on January 23, 1970; set apart as president of the Quorum of the Twelve Apostles on July 7, 1972; and ordained and set apart as president of the Church on December 30, 1973, at age seventy-eight. He passed away on November 5, 1985, at age ninety.[77]

EZRA TAFT BENSON
ORDAINED APOSTLE ON OCTOBER 7, 1943

President Ezra Taft Benson, thirteenth president of the Church, is the great-grandson of Elder Ezra Taft Benson of the Twelve, who is commonly referred to as Ezra T. Benson. President Benson notes this about his call to the Apostleship, "I was called to the Council of the Twelve thirty-three years ago this last October. The thought that I should ever occupy such a place had never entered my mind. I must confess to you, I had no premonition of the calling, and when President Grant issued the call, I could hardly believe it was true. Till that moment in my life, my consuming desire was to be an effective stake president, a position I held in the Washington Stake at the time of the call."[78]

Ezra Taft Benson was ordained an Apostle on October 7, 1943, at age forty-four, by President Heber J. Grant. In 1953 Elder Benson was called by President Dwight D. Eisenhower, thirty-fourth President of the United States, to serve as U. S. Secretary of Agriculture. With approval from President David O. McKay, ninth president of the Church, Elder Benson served in this position from 1953 to 1961. He was set apart as president of the Quorum of the Twelve Apostles on December 30, 1973; he was ordained and set apart as president of the Church on November 10, 1985, at age eighty-six. He passed away on May 30, 1994, at age ninety-four.[79]

MATTHEW COWLEY
ORDAINED APOSTLE ON OCTOBER 11, 1945

Elder Matthew Cowley is the son of Elder Matthias F. Cowley of the Twelve. Elder Matthew Cowley notes the following about his call:

Now, I remember when President Rufus K. Hardy, of the First Council of Seventy, passed away. . . .

After President Hardy died we had a memorial service for him. I'll never forget the native who was up speaking, saying what a calamity it was to the mission to lose this great New Zealand missionary who could do so much for them as one of the Authorities of the Church. He was talking along that line, and all of a sudden he stopped and he looked around at me and said, "Wait a minute. There is nothing to worry about. Not a thing to worry about. When President Cowley gets home he'll fill the first vacancy in the Council of the Twelve Apostles, and we'll still have a representative among the authorities of the Church." Then he went on talking about President Hardy. When I arrived home the following September I filled the first vacancy in the Quorum of the Twelve. Now did that just happen by chance? Oh, I might have thought so if it had been one of you white Gentiles that had prophesied that, but not from the blood of Israel. Oh no, I could not deny it, I couldn't doubt it.[80]

Matthew Cowley was ordained an Apostle on October 11, 1945, at age forty-eight, by President George Albert Smith. He passed away on December 13, 1953, at age fifty-six.[81]

HENRY DINWOODEY MOYLE
ORDAINED APOSTLE ON APRIL 10, 1947

President Henry D. Moyle, first counselor to President David O. McKay, relates the following about his call:

> I will never cease to be grateful to the Lord for the first and lasting impression he gave me in reference to my call into the circle of the General Authorities. . . . I was in New York on one of the largest legal matters that I had ever handled, and I had just barely laid the foundation for the negotiations on a Friday afternoon, with appointments for the next week, when President [George Albert] Smith called me and told me to catch

a night plane home. From that moment to this I have never been back into my old office. When I came home President George F. Richards [President of the Quorum of the Twelve Apostles] said, "I would like to see you in the morning."

He made his request at the afternoon session of the conference, and I was due back in New York—I had been promised by President Smith that I could be back to New York Monday morning. But, to make a long story short, I never went at all. I telephoned New York and told my client to pack up my bags, which I had not had time to bring with me that Friday night, and to bring them home. I informed him that he would have to start over again with somebody else. He was, of course, agreeable.

I am so grateful for that. It was not even a temptation. I had gone to President Smith just the Tuesday before. (I was then the chairman of the General Welfare Committee and had been for many years, and I was accustomed to going to conference.) I said, "Would you like to excuse me from this General Conference, or should I give up this work in New York?" And he said, "Go ahead, my boy. We have no use for you here." And so I left. So I know that between Tuesday and Friday afternoon something happened. President Smith told me what happened, and I have never had any occasion to doubt it. He said that the Lord had spoken. . . . I know with all my heart and soul what he told me was true.[82]

Giving further information about his call, President Moyle related the following:

> I went up to President George Albert Smith after he had had me sustained as a member of the Quorum of the Twelve, and I thanked him for the confidence and the love. . . . He said, "Brother Moyle, you have me to thank for nothing. I didn't call you into the Twelve. The Lord did." Now isn't that wonderful to have prophets of God tell you that there is nothing personal about your call and

to know and to have that witness given to you that you are called.... And I bear witness to you that we have it [the Priesthood] and that the apostleship has been conferred upon me as well as the Presidency with power to function and officiate in whatever assignment President McKay makes to me. And I can go forward with the fulfillment of that assignment with the knowledge that the Spirit of the Lord and His inspiration become mine. I have a right to them, and I receive them.[83]

Henry D. Moyle was ordained an Apostle on April 10, 1947, at age fifty-seven, by President George Albert Smith. He was sustained as second counselor to President David O. McKay on June 12, 1959, and sustained as first counselor to President McKay on October 12, 1961. He passed away on September 18, 1963, at age seventy-four.[84]

DELBERT LEON STAPLEY
ORDAINED APOSTLE ON OCTOBER 5, 1950

In his first talk as an Apostle, Elder Delbert L. Stapley said:

I would like to tell you just a little about the call [to the Council of the Twelve] because it is a testimony, at least to me....

Thursday, having some stake business to transact just following the noon hour, but understanding the General Authorities were in session, I thought I had time to go down the street and visit a friend of mine before they returned to their offices. As I got out of the elevator in the Hotel Utah [which is now the Joseph Smith Memorial Building, in Salt Lake City, Utah], whom should the Lord place in my path but President George Albert Smith. There is no one I would rather see, for I have known and loved him for a long time.... And so here he was, blocking my way. He said, "President Stapley, you are just the man I am looking for." There in the lobby of Hotel Utah he told me that it was the wish of the Brethren that I come on the Council. Well, I saw him to the door, and I am sure I must have looked like a ghost because people were staring at me as I walked back into the hotel.[85]

Concerning a blessing he received years earlier, he continued:

> As I was passing through Salt Lake City on my way to the Southern States Mission, I receive a patriarchal blessing from [Patriarch] Hyrum G. Smith. . . . I haven't read that blessing for some little time, but after this call came, two things in that blessing stood out. . . . One was that I would be called into positions of responsibility and trust. And this, in a measure, I have enjoyed along the way, but the crowning achievement is in this appointment to the apostleship. And the other was that I would travel much for the gospel's sake.[86]

Delbert L. Stapley was ordained an Apostle on October 5, 1950, at age fifty-three, by President George Albert Smith. He passed away on August 19, 1978, at age eighty-one.[87]

MARION GEORGE ROMNEY
ORDAINED APOSTLE ON OCTOBER 11, 1951

After being called and sustained as the first assistant to the Twelve on April 6, 1941, at age forty-three, Elder Marion G. Romney was later called as a member of the Twelve Apostles. Elder Stapley said the following about the calling of Elder Romney:

> We read in the thirteenth chapter of the Acts of the Apostles that there were in the Church at Antioch certain prophets and teachers, that among these were Barnabas and Saul. The record says,
>
> "As they ministered to the Lord, and fasted, the Holy Ghost said, Separate me Barnabas and Saul for the work whereunto I have called them." (Acts 13:2)
>
> We had occasion in the upper room of the [Salt Lake] temple the other day to witness a similar experience in the selection of Elder Romney to the Council of the Twelve. As his name was presented, there was a unanimous feeling that this man had been called of God to the important position that he now occupies.[88]

Marion G. Romney was ordained an Apostle on October 11, 1951, at age fifty-four, by President David O. McKay. He was sustained as second counselor to President Harold B. Lee on July 7, 1972; sustained as second counselor to President Spencer W. Kimball on December 30, 1973; sustained as first counselor to President Kimball on December 2, 1982; and released at the death of President Kimball on November 5, 1985, and resumed his position in the Quorum of the Twelve Apostles. He became president of the Quorum of the Twelve Apostles on November 10, 1985. He passed away on May 20, 1988, at age ninety.[89]

HUGH BROWN BROWN
ORDAINED APOSTLE ON APRIL 10, 1958

The following was written of a young Hugh B. Brown:

> A . . . missionary conference held in Bradford [England, in 1906] had a profound influence on the Canadian elder. In his mission journal he remarked, "We had the best and most spirited meeting I have ever attended. President [Heber J.] Grant spoke with great power and gave some very good instructions. Most every elder wept with joy." In his memoirs President Brown recalls that the apostle paused before closing and said, "Brethren, there is sitting in this audience someone who will someday be a member of the Council of the Twelve and I predict this in the name of Jesus Christ." Like the others, Elder Brown wondered who that might be and thought little of his own chances.
>
> When Hugh B. Brown was sustained as an Assistant to the Council of the Twelve at the general conference in October, 1953, it was a long step toward the fulfillment of a cherished dream. He had been a teenage farm boy in Spring Coulee, Alberta [Canada], when the dream was instilled in him by an incident involving his mother, Lydia, and a visitor in the Brown home, Elder Francis M. Lyman [of the Twelve]. Following the visit the apostle went to Cardston to preside at the stake conference, and the prophetic promise which ensued is remembered by President Brown as follows:
>
> "Mother and I went to conference . . . in the horse and buggy. As we were coming home she told me of an experience she had had while [Elder] Francis M. Lyman

was addressing the conference. She said: 'As I looked upon him he ceased to be Francis M. Lyman and became Hugh B. Brown and I saw you occupying the position he then held. I know as I know I live that that's what is going to happen to you. If you will just behave yourself and do what is right, the time will come when you will be called into the Council of the Twelve.'"

Several of the apostles confirmed President Grant's statement [while Brother Brown was serving a mission], and Elder John A. Widtsoe [of the Twelve] is remembered as having stated, "The time will come when you will be in that group."[90]

In the *Memoirs of Hugh B. Brown,* Elder Brown himself wrote:

> Not quite five years after I was called as an Assistant to the Twelve, a vacancy arose in the Quorum of the Twelve Apostles. Nothing was said to me about it until after one of the morning sessions of General Conference when President McKay commented to me, "I would like to see you in the office here in the Tabernacle immediately at the close of this meeting." I went into the room and met with President McKay.
>
> "The Lord wants you to be a member of the Council of the Twelve. How do you feel about it?" President McKay asked.
>
> "If ever I was justified in criticizing what the Lord wants, I am in that position now," I answered, "because I feel that I am unprepared."
>
> "'We [members of the First Presidency] don't agree with you,' he replied. "We have submitted your name to the Twelve and they have approved. Now what we want you to tell us is whether you will accept it."
>
> "Of course," I said. "I will accept any call that comes from the Lord and do the best I can with it. But as for being qualified for it, I have serious doubts."
>
> President McKay thereupon called those of the Twelve who were present in the room to join him. They surrounded me, laid their hands upon my head,

and ordained me an apostle. Later, the president gave me what is known as the "charge to the apostles." That charge included a commitment to give all that one has, both as to time and means, to the building of the Kingdom of God; to keep himself pure and unspotted from the sins of the world; to be obedient to the authorities of the church; and to exercise the freedom to speak his mind but always be willing to subjugate his own thoughts and accept the majority opinion—not only to vote for it but to act as though it were his own original opinion after it has been approved by the majority of the Council of the Twelve and the First Presidency.

After they set me apart, the matter submitted to the General Conference of the Church and I was asked to say something. I spoke for only two minutes, promising that the balance of my life would be spent trying to prove that the judgment of the brethren was justified. If I could do that I would feel that I was worthy of the call. Afterwards I wrote in my journal, "This calling was very humbling indeed but is in fulfillment of a life-long ambition of my beloved mother, who predicted it when I was but a boy."[91]

Hugh B. Brown was ordained an Apostle on April 10, 1958, at age seventy-four, by President David O. McKay. He was sustained as a counselor in the First Presidency on June 22, 1961; sustained as second counselor to President McKay on October 12, 1961; sustained as first counselor to President McKay on October 4, 1963; and released at the death of President McKay on January 18, 1970, and resumed his position in the Quorum of the Twelve Apostles. He passed away on December 2, 1975, at age ninety-two.[92]

GORDON BITNER HINCKLEY
ORDAINED APOSTLE OCTOBER 5, 1961

President Gordon B. Hinckley is the beloved fifteenth president of the Church. After being called to serve in the European Mission, headquartered in London, England, in 1933, young Elder Hinckley read his patriarchal blessing, which he "received at age eleven from patriarch Thomas E. Callister." In his blessing, he was told:

> Thou shalt grow to the full stature of manhood and shall become a mighty and valiant leader in the midst of Israel ... Thou shalt ever be a messenger of peace; the nations of the earth shall hear thy voice and be brought to a knowledge of the truth by the wonderful testimony which thou shalt bear. Perhaps, he thought, this mission to England would fulfill at least one part of his blessing—that he would bear testimony to the nations (England and the United States being a plurality) of the earth.[93]

Then, twenty-eight years later the following happened:

> At 7:00 A.M. on Saturday, September 30, 1961, the phone rang in the white frame house in East Millcreek [in Salt Lake City, Utah]. Marjorie [the wife of Elder Hinckley] answered to find President [David O.] McKay on the other end of the line. Might he speak to Gordon? ... [When he spoke to Brother Hinckley, he asked:] "Could you come to my office as soon as possible?"
>
> Less than an hour later the two men sat knee to knee and President McKay explained the reason for this early visit prior to that morning's session of general conference: "I have felt to nominate you to fill the vacancy in the Quorum of the Twelve Apostles," he told Elder Hinckley simply, "and we would like to sustain you today in conference." The words took Gordon's breath away, and he searched without success for a response. How could it be, that such a call would come to him? He had known, of course, of the vacancy in the Quorum [created in June when President Hugh B. Brown had been called to serve as a third counselor in the First Presidency]. But never for a moment had he—or would he have—thought he would be called to fill it.[94]

Gordon B. Hinckley was sustained as an assistant to the Twelve on April 6, 1958 and was ordained an Apostle on October 5, 1961, at age fifty-one, by President David O. McKay. He was called as a counselor to President Spencer W. Kimball on July 23, 1981, and as second counselor to President Kimball on December 2, 1982, serving until November 5, 1985. He served as first counselor to President Ezra Taft Benson from November 10, 1985, to May 30, 1994; he served as first counselor to President Howard W. Hunter from June 5, 1994 to March 3, 1995. He was ordained and set apart as the president of the Church on March 12, 1995.[95]

CHAPTER 11

MEETING THE NEEDS OF THE GROWING CHURCH

ASSISTANTS TO THE TWELVE

When the Church was organized on Tuesday, April 6, 1830, there were six official members—Joseph Smith, Oliver Cowdery, Hyrum Smith, Peter Whitmer Jr., David Whitmer, and Samuel H. Smith.[1] By December 31, 1940, there were 862,664 members worldwide.[2] At that time there were 134 stakes, 1,191 wards and branches, 35 missions, and 728 branches in those missions.[3]

At the April 1941 general conference of the Church, President J. Reuben Clark Jr., first counselor to President Heber J. Grant, spoke these significant words, "In the past history of the Church, especially in President Brigham Young's time, it was found necessary for the First Presidency or the Twelve, or both, to call brethren, frequently designated as Counselors, to help carry on their assigned work in the Church."[4]

As was presented in Chapter 9, Daniel H. Wells and John W. Young were sustained as counselors to the Twelve Apostles. In addition, Sylvester Q. Cannon was sustained as an associate to the Quorum of the Twelve Apostles.[5] With this information, we return to President Clark's words:

> The rapid growth of the Church in recent times, the constantly increasing establishment of new Wards and Stakes, the ever widening geographical area covered by Wards and Stakes, the steadily pressing necessity for increasing our missions in numbers and efficiency that the Gospel may be brought to all men [and women], the

continual multiplying of Church interests and activities calling for more rigid and frequent observation, supervision, and direction—all have built up an apostolic service of the greatest magnitude.

The First Presidency and Twelve feel that to meet adequately their great responsibilities and to carry on efficiently this service for the Lord, they should have some help.

Accordingly it has been decided to appoint Assistants to the Twelve, who shall be High Priests, who shall be set apart to act under the direction of the Twelve in the performance of such work as the First Presidency and the Twelve may place upon them.

There will be no fixed number of these Assistants. Their number will be increased or otherwise from time to time as the necessity of carrying on the Lord's work seems to dictate to be wise.

It is proposed that we sustain as Assistants to the Twelve, the following named High Priests, who will labor under the supervision and direction of the First Presidency and of the Twelve.

Marion G. Romney, President of Bonneville Stake.

Thomas E. McKay [brother of President David O. McKay, then Second Counselor to President Heber J. Grant], former President of Ogden Stake and Acting President of the European Mission.

Clifford E. Young, President of the Alpine Stake.

Alma Sonne, President of Cache Stake.

Nicholas G. Smith, President of the Northwestern States Mission.[6]

A Church publication added the following:

President Heber J. Grant, the Prophet, Seer, and Revelator. . . holding the keys of the kingdom, selected five brethren to be Assistants to the Twelve Apostles.

[They were] then sustained by the body of the Church at a general conference as *General Authorities* and Assistants to the Quorum of the Twelve.[7]

From this information, we learn that President Grant was inspired by the Lord to call the five men mentioned, and they were sustained to be General Authorities in The Church of Jesus Christ of Latter-day Saints.

As was written, Marion G. Romney was the first assistant to the Twelve called. Concerning his call, we read his informative words:

> I remember when I was called to the General Authorities, I was the first Assistant to the Twelve named. I was practicing law at that time. I went up to the [Salt Lake] Tabernacle one morning to [General] Conference, I think it was on a Saturday morning. I was sitting in the audience between Dr. Gleave, who was a member of our High Council, and my second counselor, Oren Jacobsen, and I heard them read off the names of the General Authorities. There was a vacancy in the Council of the Twelve and they read off the name of Harold B. Lee to fill that vacancy. He had been a good friend of ours [my wife and I] for years. We had met in each other's homes in a little Church History group back and forth, and so we were elated. And Brother Clark went on reading, and he said something that was a little unusual in the routine in maintaining the Authorities for the action of the people, and he said something about like this: "Now this isn't a quote, but it's a thought, that from time to time in the Church, the Apostolic Service had grown to a point where the General Authorities needed some help and they had called into the service, men to help them." Sometimes this additional help was for the Presidency, and sometimes for the Council of the Twelve, and now the work had reached that condition again, and so they were calling five High Priests to be known as "Assistants to the Council of the Twelve." "It is therefore proposed that we sustain as Assistants to the Council of the Twelve, Marion G. Romney . . ." and that's the last name I heard, but I learned afterwards that he had named Brothers Thomas E. McKay, Clifford E. Young, Alma Sonne, and Nicholas G. Smith.
>
> Well, they didn't tell us what our call was, that is, what we were to do. I went back to my law office and we [all five

men] wondered what we were going to do and they kept us wondering for quite a while. . . . President Clark invited us to his house. Five of us to a dinner, and he talked to us and he asked me how I felt about it and I told him that I felt terrible about being in suspense, not knowing what I was called to do, and he said that it was a good purifying experience for me to go through. And then my wife and I used to talk about it and we were wondering what they were going to have us do, and one day she said, "I think I know what they'll have you do!" I asked, "You do?" and I said, "What?" She said, "I think they'll have you go down and help Harold." That was Brother Lee [recently called as a member of the Twelve], who had been managing director of the Welfare Program from the time it started when he and Brother [Melvin J.] Ballard [of the Twelve] went around the Church, you remember, organizing the Welfare Program. And I said, "Oh, my heavens! I hope not. There's no place in the Church that I wouldn't rather work." The next day I received a letter signed by all three members of the Presidency [President Heber J. Grant; J. Reuben Clark Jr. First Counselor; and David O. McKay, Second Counselor]. I don't know how my wife found this out before I did, but, sure enough, I was called to report down to the office of Brother Harold B. Lee and work with him. I was to be the Assistant Managing Director of the Welfare Program.

Well, that was way back in August or September of 1941. I was called in as an Assistant to the Twelve in the April Conference in 1941 and then I went to work [five to six months later].[8]

In 1956, the following duties were written:

The Assistants . . . at the present time are assigned to perform many of the tasks which the Twelve Apostles are assigned to do. They function as General Authorities of the Church in conducting stake conferences, in touring missions, in ordaining bishoprics, and in approving and setting apart presidencies of high priests' quorums.

They assist the Apostles in reorganizing stakes. They also interview prospective missionaries and recommend them for calls to missions. They co-operate with the First Council of Seventy by ordaining seventies [in stakes and wards] and setting apart presidencies of seventies' quorums. They also receive assignments to perform temple marriages, and other such special assignments as the First Presidency may desire to give them. . . .

[Note these words:] The Assistants to the Twelve Apostles do not constitute a quorum in the priesthood. . . . they do not hold special meetings as a body of the priesthood.

The Assistants . . . attend the meetings of the General Authorities. . . .

Thus in every way in accordance with their scope of assignments, they are helping to regulate and administer the activities of the Church.[9]

From April 6, 1941, to October 1, 1976, a total of thirty-eight men were called and sustained as assistants to the Twelve. In 1976, the First Presidency dispensed with this calling, and those members then serving were sustained to the First Quorum of the Seventy on October 1, 1976. It is significant to emphasize that from the thirty-eight men called as assistants to the Twelve Apostles, thirteen were called and sustained as members of the Quorum of the Twelve Apostles. They are as follows:

    Marion G. Romney—1st assistant
    George Q. Morris—6th assistant
    Hugh B. Brown—10th assistant
    Gordon B. Hinckley—12th assistant
    N. Eldon Tanner—16th assistant
    Boyd K. Packer—20th assistant
    Marvin J. Ashton—24th assistant
    David B. Haight—26th assistant
    James E. Faust—31st assistant
    L. Tom Perry—32nd assistant
    Neal A. Maxwell—34th assistant
    Robert D. Hales—36th assistant
    Joseph B. Wirthlin—the last and 38th assistant[10]

Release of Assistants to the Twelve; Quorums of the Seventy Established

To meet the needs of the growing Church, the First Presidency and the Quorum of the Twelve considered the proper role of the Seventy. "Their concern came at a time when, even with the combined support groups of the Assistants to the Twelve, Regional Representatives, and the Seventy, they were taxed to the limit in administering what had become a worldwide church."[11]

Traditionally, the order of the priesthood was deacon, teacher, priest, elder, seventy, high priest, Seventy, Apostle. After being assigned, and laboring in faith, Elder Boyd K. Packer's diligent efforts of studying verses in D&C 107 helped, he and his fellow Brethren to determine how the Lord intended it to be "with the Seventy being listed only once."[12]

"In perfect unity the Twelve presented their recommendations to the First Presidency. After much prayer and deliberation, the prophet [President Spencer W. Kimball] and his Counselors began to implement orderly changes relative to the Seventy. On 1 October 1976 the First Quorum of the Seventy was expanded by the release of all twenty-one Assistants to the Twelve and their call as Seventies, and by the calling of four new Seventies."[13]

Accordingly, the Seventy was not a local priesthood call; it was that Seventy which "form a quorum equal in authority to that of the Twelve special witnesses or Apostles" (see D&C 107:26). Therefore, all stake seventies were released at the time the Quorum of Seventy was reorganized on the general Church level. This was a huge moment for those who were stake seventies at that time—and, it was a significant organizational change for the Church.

"On 1 April 1989 the organization of the Second Quorum of the Seventy was announced. It was comprised of thirty-six members who were called to serve five years."[14]

Regional Representatives of the Twelve

Men called to be regional representatives of the Twelve were assigned by the Quorum of the Twelve Apostles and the First Presidency to advance and administer the work of the Church. In 1995, President Hinckley said, "They have greatly assisted stake presidents and bishops with wise counsel and direction, with skillful training and instruction." President Hinckley also said:

> Twenty-eight years ago the First Presidency was inspired to call men to serve as regional representatives of the Twelve. At the time that was a new calling in the Church. The Presidency stated that this was necessary because of "the ever-increasing growth of the Church" which made "evident a greater need to train our stake and ward leaders in the programs of the Church that they in turn might train the membership in their responsibilities before the Lord."
>
> At that time there were 69 regional representatives. Today there are 284. The organization has become somewhat unwieldy. . . .
>
> It is now felt desirable to tighten up the organization administered by the area presidencies. Accordingly, we announce the release—the honorable release—of all regional representatives effective August 15 of this year.[15]

Another publication notes, "The position of Regional Representatives of the Twelve was announced September 29, 1967. . . . The position was eliminated with the calling of Area Authorities on April 1, 1995."[16]

In speaking of regional representatives, President Hinckley emphasized this doctrine, "Now in the ongoing of this work, administrative changes sometimes occur. The doctrine remains constant. But from time to time there are organizational and administrative changes made under provisions set forth in the revelations."[17]

Concerning one of those revelations, it is written:

> Of the Melchizedek Priesthood, three Presiding High Priests, chosen by the body, appointed and ordained to that office, and upheld by the confidence, faith, and prayer of the church, form a quorum of the Presidency of the Church.
>
> The twelve traveling councilors are called to be the Twelve Apostles . . . And they form a quorum, equal in authority and power to the three presidents previously mentioned.
>
> The Seventy are also called to preach the gospel, and to be especial witnesses . . .

> And they form a quorum, equal in authority to that of the Twelve special witnesses or Apostles just named" (D& C 107:22–26).

Now, notice the words *decision* and *decisions* in these next verses:

> The *decisions* of these quorums, or either of them, are to be made in all righteousness (D&C 107:30; italics added for emphasis).
>
> And in case that any *decision* of these quorums is made in unrighteousness, it may be brought before a general assembly of the several quorums, which constitute the spiritual authorities of the church; otherwise there can be no appeal from their decision" (D&C 107:32; emphasis added)

Therefore, it is written, "Because the promise is, if these things [meaning: righteous decisions] abound in them [the presiding quorums of the Church] they shall not be unfruitful in the knowledge of the Lord" (D&C 107:31).

We can see that the full organization of the Church was not revealed from the beginning. As Church membership has increased, the Twelve Apostles and First Presidency have sought and received direction from the Lord to meet the needs of the growing Church.

CHAPTER 12

THE TWELVE ARE CHOSEN TO BE SPECIAL WITNESSES

TRIAL OR PURIFYING OF THE TWELVE

Every person who is born on this earth is subjected to trials, which includes opposition, hardship, suffering, temptation, and death. In the Book of Mormon, Lehi expounds this great truth when he teaches, "For it must needs be, that there is an opposition in all things. If not so . . . righteousness could not be brought to pass, neither wickedness, neither holiness nor misery, neither good nor bad" (2 Nephi 2:11). Later, he writes these truth-filled words: "Wherefore, men [and women] are free according to the flesh . . . And they are free to choose liberty and eternal life, through the great Mediator [Jesus Christ] of all men, or to choose captivity and death, according to the captivity and power of the devil; for he seeketh that all men might be miserable like unto himself" (2 Nephi 2:27).

Specifically speaking to those who belong to The Church of Jesus Christ of Latter-day Saints, the Lord says, "My people must be tried in all things, that they may be prepared to receive the glory that I have for them, even the glory of Zion; and he [or she] that will not bear chastisement is not worthy of my kingdom" (see D&C 136:31).

By way of introduction, Elder Harold B. Lee made this significant statement:

> We must expect opposition, and sometimes that opposition may come from inside, but remember what the Prophet Joseph Smith our early leader said: "The nearer a person approaches the Lord, the greater the

power will be manifested by the Adversary to prevent the accomplishment of his purposes." One of the brethren, President John Taylor, said he heard the Prophet say, "You have all kinds of trials to pass through, and it is quite as necessary for you to be tried even as Abraham, and other men of God," and said he, "God will feel after you, he will take hold of you and wrench your very heartstrings, and if you cannot stand it you will not be fit for an inheritance in the Kingdom of God."[1]

In harmony with these remarks, Elder Marion G. Romney of the Twelve said, "I have seen the remorse and despair in the lives of men who, in the hour of trial, have cursed God and died spiritually. And I have seen people rise to great heights from what seemed to be unbearable burdens. Finally, I have sought the Lord in my own extremities and learned for myself that my soul has made its greatest growth as I have been driven to my knees by adversity and affliction."[2]

What is a trial to one individual may not be to another. There are people who struggle with living the Word of Wisdom, while others find it easy to observe. Some struggle with paying tithing, while others faithfully pay a tenth of their annual increase. The list can go on. Speaking by the Spirit, Elder George Q. Cannon revealed this doctrine, when he said, "God is going to have a tried people, and the trials will not always come in the form that we are looking for . . . but they come in forms for which, it may be said, we are partly unprepared. They come to us in unexpected forms; therefore the greater the trial of our faith."[3]

Mortality is full of trials and opposition. Though some wonder why they have to experience trials and challenges, they are a necessary part in the eternal plan of salvation (see 2 Nephi 2:11, 15–16). Individuals can face trials and opposition with faith and courage or the lack of it. In reference to Church leaders, President Joseph F. Smith spoke these encouraging words:

> Leaders must be courageous. One of the highest qualities of all true leadership is a high standard of courage. When we speak of courage and leadership we are using terms that stand for the quality of life by which men determine consciously the proper course to pursue and stand with fidelity to their convictions. There has

never been a time in the Church when its leaders were not required to be courageous men; not alone courageous in the sense that they were able to meet physical dangers, but also in the sense that they were steadfast and true to a clear and upright conviction.

Leaders of the Church, then, should be men not easily discouraged, not without hope, and not given to forebodings of all sorts of evils to come. Above all things the leaders of the people should never disseminate a spirit of gloom in the hearts of the people. If men standing in high places sometimes feel the weight and anxiety of momentous times, they should be all the firmer and all the more resolute in those convictions which come from a God-fearing conscience and pure lives. Men in their private lives should feel the necessity of extending encouragement to the people by their own hopeful and cheerful intercourse with them, as they do by their utterances in public places. It is a matter of the greatest importance that the people be educated to appreciate and cultivate the bright side of life rather than to permit its darkness and shadows to hover over them.[4]

FORMS OF TRIAL OR PURIFYING

Members of the Council of the Twelve go through various forms of trial or purifying. Some have this experience prior to or shortly after their call. We are most fortunate that some of the Brethren have written or spoken about their personal trial or purifying. We begin with remarks from President Brigham Young:

> When the Quorum of the Twelve was first organized, [the Prophet] Joseph said that the Elders of Israel, and particularly the Twelve Apostles, would receive more temptations, be more buffeted, and have greater difficulty to escape the evil thrown in their way by females than by any other means. This is one of Satan's most powerful auxiliaries with which to weaken the influence of the ministers of Christ, and bring them down from their high position and calling into darkness, shame, and

disgrace. You will have to guard more strictly against that than against any other evil that may beset you.[5]

In conjunction with this, Elder Francis M. Lyman of the Twelve said, "Under strict instructions from our file leaders we carefully avoid all familiarity with women. The occasional misfortunes of some of our fellow missionaries were standing warnings to us to avoid the very appearance of evil."[6]

With this stated, our attention now turns to a test of loyalty. Specifically speaking of members of the Quorum of the Twelve Apostles, Elder Harold B. Lee revealed the following:

> I have listened to the classic stories in this dispensation about how Brigham Young was tested, how Heber C. Kimball was tested, John Taylor and Willard Richards in Carthage Jail, Zion's Camp that received a great test, and from that number were chosen the first General Authorities in this dispensation. There were others who didn't pass the test of loyalty, and they fell from their places.
>
> I have been in a position since I came into the Council of the Twelve to observe some things among my brethren, and I want to say to you: Every man my junior in the Council of the Twelve, I have seen submitted as though by providence, to these same tests of loyalty, and I wondered sometimes whether they were going to pass the tests. The reason they are here today is because they did, and our Father [in Heaven] has honored them.
>
> I have that same witness about at least two members of the Assistants to the Twelve, Brother Marion G. Romney and Brother Alma Sonne, for I saw it, and I know the nature of the test, and I know how they proved themselves to be the sterling men that they are. And so God has honored them, and it is my conviction that every man who will be called to a high place in this Church will have to pass these tests not devised by human hands, by which our Father [in Heaven] numbers them as a united group of leaders willing to follow the prophets of the Living God and be loyal and true as witnesses and exemplars of the truths they teach.[7]

Giving a specific example, Elder Lee continued:

> Brigham Young in his day was invited into a group of some of those who were trying to argue against that principle of unity. After he learned that they were trying to "dispose" as they said, the Prophet Joseph Smith, he stood before them and said something like this: "You cannot destroy the appointment of a prophet of God, but you can cut the thread which binds you to a prophet of God and sink yourselves to hell."
>
> It was that kind of fearlessness which was manifest in him that made him the peerless leader he was to become. It is that same kind of courage, though not always popular, but the kind that has been demanded of every man whom our Father [in Heaven] would honor with high places of leadership.[8]

Five years later, Elder Lee expressed the following about his call to the Apostleship:

> It was the day when I was ordained to my present calling, where my wife and I were invited to the home of one of the brethren for a social evening with others of the First Presidency and the Council of the Twelve. . . . As a part of the evening's entertainment, if that it could be called, each member of the Presidency and the Twelve were asked to recite their experience in being called into the Council of the Twelve or the Presidency. I was amazed as I sat listening to the brethren, beginning with the President and so on through the Twelve, that each was telling my story. They were telling the experience that I at that moment was going through, or had gone through. [Note these words] Then again I began to realize that all must be tested and tried and that there is a certain refinement that is necessary before one qualifies to the highest station to which the Lord would have him called.[9]

Concerning a refinement process, Elder Richard L. Evans of the Twelve shared a portion of Elder Spencer W. Kimball's story:

> With all the confidence he has in his mission, yet upon his call to the Council of the Twelve, Brother Kimball was beset with doubts and inner worries—not doubts as to the work, but as to his own ability and powers. Between July 18, 1943, when President [J. Reuben] Clark [Jr.], speaking for President [Heber J.] Grant [seventh President of the Church], telephoned him from Salt Lake City to tell him that he had been called to the Council of the Twelve—between then and when he was sustained and set apart after the general conference in October [1943], he underwent an intense inner adjustment of which perhaps no one who has not been through it can quite conceive—three months of sensitive, acute self-searching—like Paul in his Arabian preparation for his ministry—followed by a determination to dedicate his life to the call that had come to him. And that he has done.[10]

In addition to this experience of purifying, Elder Boyd K. Packer writes about Elder Kimball's experience with the power of evil:

> On two occasions, each time when he was on assignments to stake quarterly conference, and each time not related to problems incident to the conference, there was unleashed against him the very might of the adversary. He endured during those hours, not to be recorded here, something akin to what his grandfather [Elder Heber C. Kimball] had experienced when, as an Apostle of the Lord, he opened the work in England, something not unlike the Prophet Joseph experienced as he first knelt in the Grove. These trials have made him humbly dependent upon the power of the Lord.[11]

Our attention also turns to a trial that Elder Hugh B. Brown experienced:

> We were in Canada. I was . . . an attorney for an oil company and a manager of it. We were drilling wells and making money. I was at the moment up in the Canadian

Rockies, way back from the highways. We were drilling there. Everything looked very prosperous.

I woke very early one morning before daylight. I was troubled in my mind, and I didn't know the source or the reason for the trouble. And I began to pray, but didn't seem to get an answer. And I . . . went back into the hills where I knew no one would be near. And when I got up on an advantageous point, I began to talk out loud. I was talking to God! Now, I do not mean that he was standing there listening to me or replying to me. But I mean from the very center of my heart I was calling to him.

Now my family were all in good health, all quite prosperous, and it looked as for myself that within a few days I would be a multi-millionaire. And yet, I was depressed. And up there on that mountain peak I said to him, "O God, if what it seems is about to happen will happen, and if it is not to be for the best good of myself and my family and my friends, don't let it happen. Take it from me," I said, "Don't let it happen unless in your wisdom it is good for me." Well, I left the mountains and came down to the camp. I got into my car and drove to the city of Edmonton. It was a Friday, and while I was driving I was thinking of what had happened. And I felt that there was something impending that I couldn't understand. When I arrived home, and after a bite to eat, I said to Sister Brown, "I think I'll occupy the back bedroom because I'm afraid I'm not going to sleep." Now I went in the bedroom alone and there, through the night, I had the most terrible battle with the powers of the adversary. I wanted to destroy myself. Not in the sense of suicide; but something within me was impelling me to wish that I could cease to be . . . it was terrible. The blackness was so thick you could feel it.

Sister Brown came in later in the night, toward morning in fact, wanting to know what was the matter. And when she closed the door, she said, "What's in this room?'" And I said, "Nothing but the power of the devil is in this room." And we knelt together by the bedside and prayed for release. We spent the night together, the balance of it. And in the morning I went down to my office. It was Saturday now and there was no one at the office. And in going into the office, I knelt by a cot and asked God for deliverance from the darkness that had enveloped me. And coming from somewhere there was an element of peace, the kind of peace that rests on the souls of men when they make contact with God.

That night at 10:00 o'clock, October 1953—the telephone rang. Sister Brown answered. She called me and said, "Salt Lake's calling," and I wondered who could be calling me from that far away. I took the phone and said, "Hello." "This is [President] David O. McKay calling. The Lord wants you to give the balance of your life to Him and His Church [as an Assistant to the Twelve Apostles]. We are in a conference of the Church. The concluding session will be tomorrow afternoon. Can you get here?"

I told him I couldn't get there because there were no planes flying, but I would get there as soon as possible. I knew that a call had come. [Note these words] And the call came after this awful conflict with the adversary. And when he [President McKay] said,

"The Lord wants you to give the balance of your life to the Church," I knew that it meant giving up the money; it meant that I'd turn everything over to someone else and go to Salt Lake without monetary remuneration.

Since that time, I've been happier than ever before in my life. The men with whom I was associated have made millions [of dollars]. And yet, when one of them was in my office not long ago in Salt Lake, he said, "I am worth at least seven million dollars. I would gladly give every dollar of it to you if you could give me what you have. I can't buy it with money, but I'd like to have what you have. What you have is peace of soul, and I cannot buy that with money."

Brothers and sisters, I leave this testimony with you.[12]

We now turn to a purifying experience of Elder N. Eldon Tanner:

> President McKay told me that the Lord wanted me to come and work with him and the other General Authorities as an Assistant to the Twelve. As I expressed myself in the morning session, I could only bear my testimony and commit myself to the call . . .
>
> Following the conference, I spent many sleepless nights with a feeling of weeping inside and many nights I had a wet pillow. I understand what it meant to have a broken heart and contrite spirit, because I felt that a cleansing had been going on for several days to prepare me to perform the duties expected of me.[13]

LEADERS NEVER CLAIM INFALLIBILITY

The following was written by Brother Charles W. Penrose in 1880. Fourteen years later, he was ordained an Apostle on July 7, 1904, at age seventy-two.

> The authorities of The Church of Jesus Christ of Latter-day Saints have never laid claim to infallibility [Meaning they are incapable of error or making error in defining doctrines touching faith and morals]. They have never pretended to be anything but mortal men, liable to error, subject to the common infirmities of frail humanity. They do claim to have received Divine authority to administer in the name of the Most High God. And the people associated with them as brethren and sisters in the Church recognize that authority as valid and legitimate. Does that make the men holding it infallible? Certainly not. Moses was a prophet of God and was divinely authorized to lead Israel from bondage. Was he therefore infallible? Not at all, but lost the right to enter the Promised Land through his folly. A modern Moses, with similar gifts and authority, would, because of them, be no more infallible than the ancient Moses. He would be simply a man with a mission and legitimate authority to perform his work in the name of Deity. Either Moses will be judged like

any other mortal, according to his works, viewed by his light and opportunities.

None of the leaders of this Church pretend to infallibility. Truth is infallible and comes from an infallible Being, but flows often through fallible channels or instruments.[14]

In reference to the senior Apostle, who is the president of the Church, Elder Boyd K. Packer observed, "Some time ago a historian gave a lecture to an audience of college students on one of the past Presidents of the Church. It seemed to be his purpose to show that that President was a man subject to the foibles [minor flaws or shortcomings] of men. He introduced many so-called facts that put that President in a very unfavorable light, particularly when they were taken out of the context of the historical period in which he lived."[15]

Later, Elder Packer says:

> What the historian did with the reputation of the President of the Church was not worth doing. He seemed determined to convince everyone that the Prophet was a man. We knew that already. All of the prophets and all of the apostles have been men. It would have been much more worthwhile for him to convince us that the man was a prophet, a fact quite as true as the fact that he was a man.
>
> He [this historian] has taken something away from the memory of a prophet. He has destroyed faith.
>
> The sad thing is that he may have, in years past, taken great interest in those who led the Church and desired to draw close to them. But instead of following that long, steep, discouraging, and occasionally dangerous path to spiritual achievement, instead of going up to where they were [note these words], he devised a way of collecting mistakes and weaknesses and limitations to compare with his own. In that sense he has attempted to bring a historical figure down to his level and in that way feel close to him and perhaps justify his own weaknesses. . . .
>
> That historian or scholar who delights in pointing out the weaknesses and frailties of present or past leaders

destroys faith. [Note this prophetic warning] A destroyer of faith—particularly one within the Church, and more particularly one who is employed specifically to build faith—places himself in great spiritual jeopardy. He is serving the wrong master, and unless he repents, he will not be among the faithful in the eternities.[16]

SWEETEST ASSOCIATIONS

When an individual is called to be a member of the Quorum of the Twelve Apostles, he enters into a special brotherhood. In the words of President Ezra Taft Benson, then president of the Twelve, "May I say to Elder L. Tom Perry, the new member of the Twelve, you are entering one of the sweetest associations among men this side of heaven."[17]

According to a dictionary definition, the word *sweet* is defined, among others things, as marked by gentle good humor or kindliness, or a pleasant or gratifying experience.

With this understanding, read the words of President James E. Faust, second counselor in the First Presidency: "We welcome Brother [Dieter F.] Uchtdorf and Brother [David A.] Bednar, men of strength and faith, into the sweet councils of the Quorum of the Twelve Apostles."[18]

To explain, in part, how sweet this association is, listen to the words of Elder Spencer W. Kimball, spoken to an assembly of missionaries:

> We have Testimony Meetings, we of the Twelve. Every three months in the [Salt Lake] Temple the Twelve sit all day long like we have today, only not quite so late because there aren't so many of us; but we go in at 8:30 a.m. and we stay until we all are through with what we want to say. We bear testimony and we tell each other how we love each other just like all of you did today. Why does the Twelve need a testimony meeting? The same reason that you need a testimony meeting. Don't you think that you can go three, and six, and nine months and twelve months without bearing your testimony and still keep its full value. . . .
>
> We have another Testimony meeting. Twice a year the First Presidency of the Church calls a testimony meeting; and all of the Presidency, and the Twelve . . . all the General Authorities . . . we all meet and hold

> in our temple robes in the upper room in the Temple a testimony meeting. We fast as we were today. We put on our temple robes. We partake of the sacrament which two of us administer and two of us pass. We pray around the circle . . . Then we bear our testimonies—not all of us—but some representatives of each group; and then all three of the Presidency of the Church express their testimonies. My good brethren and sisters, if you ever felt a thrill in your life, listen to the testimonies of the General Authorities.
>
> Do you know what they say in those testimonials? They say exactly what you have said today. There isn't anything else to say, is there?[19]

When members of the Twelve Apostles and the First Presidency bear their testimony in general conference, the Spirit manifests the truth of their words to the members of the Church. One can imagine how hearing their testimonies in the Salt Lake Temple would touch the hearts of every General Authority present. It certainly would be a *thrill* to listen to these spiritual giants bear testimony, in one of the sweetest associations among men this side of heaven.

President N. Eldon Tanner, of the First Presidency, added this information about these Thursday meetings, "Following each Thursday meeting the First Presidency and Quorum of the Twelve have lunch in a room assigned for that purpose [in the Salt Lake Temple]. In this room we have a lovely picture of the Last Supper. This is a period of relaxation, and in conversation we exchange experiences and discuss matters of common interest. I could tell you some interesting discussions if I had the time."[20]

Finally, Elder Spencer W. Kimball commented on the subject of seniority within this extraordinary group:

> Brother [Harold B.] Lee is my senior [in the Council of the Twelve], and I am Brother [Mark E.] Petersen's senior. When we go to work together, he [Elder Lee] never says, "You do this, and you can't do this." Brother Lee always say, "Now, Brother Kimball, what do you think about this? Shall we proceed along this line; shall we go here; and what shall we do there?" Always. He never tells me what I must do. When Brother Petersen

and I go, I try to do the same: "Now, Brother Petersen, shall we move in this direction; what shall we do? How do you feel about this?" It works out perfectly, and everyone is happy. But there is the senior element. When one of us is senior, someone has to take the responsibility; someone has to lead out. And that is all that it is . . . the one leads out in suggesting![21]

In life, it is enjoyable visiting with close and dear friends. The members of the Twelve become exceptionally close and dear friends. They freely discuss matters of common interest. These chosen men treat one another with great kindness and admiration. When they work together, they lead out in suggesting. They do not demean one another; they do not use vulgar language or tell inappropriate jokes or stories. They are some of the most righteous men on this earth. Their individual wit and wisdom are welcomed in any setting or meeting. Therefore, a man who is called by the Lord to be an Apostle truly enters into the sweet councils of the Quorum of the Twelve Apostles.

A Changed Man

Speaking to the members of the Church, President George Q. Cannon of the First Presidency, revealed the following:

> Let a man be ordained to the office of a Bishop or a Bishop's counselor or a High Counselor, and in every instance, if he be a faithful man, the spirit, power and gifts of his office will rest upon him. He will be filled with the same spirit which inspires the Prophet of God and those associated with him.
>
> So with an Apostle. Let the Lord select a man out of the body of the people and make him an Apostle and what a change takes place! The spirit of the Apostleship rests upon him; the gifts of that Priesthood and calling descend upon him, and he becomes a changed man in consequence of the bestowal of those powers upon him. He receives authority; he enjoys the spirit of revelation; he is upheld by the people as a Prophet, Seer and Revelator. If he is a faithful man, he receives the gift and power of a Prophet and a Revelator and perhaps of a

Seer. These are his rights, because he has been ordained to that office; and God has promised that if men will serve and obey Him in all things, He will give them the necessary power and gifts.[22]

President Ezra Taft Benson, president of the Twelve Apostles, shared thoughts that are in harmony with this statement when he said:

> Among the late members of the Twelve with whom I have served were: Elders George F. Richards, Stephen L. Richards, John A. Widtsoe, Joseph F. Merrill, Charles A. Callis, Albert E. Bowen, Matthew Cowley, Henry D. Moyle, Adam S. Bennion, Richard L. Evans, George Q. Morris, and Hugh B. Brown. I have witnessed the refining processes [of these twelve chosen men] through which the Lord chips, buffs, and polishes those whom He has selected to hold the keys of His Kingdom, that they become [changed and] polished shafts in His hand.
>
> This is particularly true in the case of those who have become presidents of the Church.
>
> Each president has been uniquely selected for the time and situation which the world and Church needed. All were "men of the hour," as we have witnessed in President [Spencer W.] Kimball [the twelfth President of the Church]. Contemplate the miracle of that foreordination and preparation! Though called and given keys many years prior to the time that the mantle fell upon him, the President was always the right man in the right place for the times. This miracle alone is one of the marks of the divinity of the Church.[23]

A CALL TO TRAVEL

The call to be a member of the Quorum of the Twelve Apostles is a call to travel. In reference to this, Elder Spencer W. Kimball spoke these informative words: "The work is changing and we have a bigger world. The members of the Council of the Twelve probably travel more today in a single week than Peter and his associates traveled in their entire lives! Yet our responsibility is the same."[24]

The life-story of Elder Boyd K. Packer provides specific examples of this call to travel. "During the thirty-plus years of his ministry, Elder Packer has been to each of the United States, to Canadian provinces, to Mexico, to countries in Central and South America, to Scandinavia and the countries of Europe, to Israel, the Middle East, Egypt, African countries, Pakistan, India, Thailand, Japan, Korea, the Philippines and the Islands of the Pacific, and to New Zealand and Australia. In so traveling he and his brethren have had their share of [good and bad] experiences."[25]

TEACHING BY SATELLITE BROADCASTS

Recently, the First Presidency and members of the Twelve have been using satellite broadcasts to teach the members of the Church. This teaching is in addition to general conferences that are broadcast in April and October of each year. While it is true that the leaders of the Church still travel to meet with members in various locations, the Brethren are taking advantage of technology to meet the needs of the growing Church. These satellite broadcasts will only increase because of the rapid growth of the Church throughout the world. With a satellite broadcast, a whole region of stakes can be instructed in one setting, instead of having a member of the Twelve or First Presidency meet personally with only one stake at a time. Truly, this technology and teaching method is inspired by the Lord.

PREDICTION OR PROPHECY FROM AN APOSTLE

As a chosen servant of the Lord, an Apostle is entitled to inspiration and revelation from the Lord. One aspect of this is the prediction of an Apostle. President Heber J. Grant said, "You need have no fear that when one of the Apostles of the Lord Jesus Christ delivers a prophecy in the name of Jesus Christ, because he is inspired to do that, that it will fall by the wayside. I know of more than one prophesy, which, looking at it naturally, seemed as though it would fall to the ground as year after year passed, but lo and behold, in the providence of the Lord, that prophecy was fulfilled."[26]

As mentioned earlier in Chapter 10 of this work, various individuals called to the Council of the Twelve were told either in a prediction or prophesy that they would become an Apostle. Though several years passed before the actual call was issued, these pronouncements were literally fulfilled over and over again.

Elder Hugh B. Brown made one of these predictions.

"In his taped memoirs President Brown recalls the impact of Pearl Harbor [a naval station attacked without warning by the Japanese on December 7, 1941].

"A letter to Mary [a daughter] two days after Pearl Harbor described the situation in more optimistic terms. 'Here in the "war zone" we are all feeling fine and itching to get at the enemy,' he wrote. (Thirty years later Hugh B. Brown would tour Japan and predict that a Japanese Latter-day Saint would one day be in the Quorum of the Twelve Apostles.)"[27]

"Some of you listening to me tonight will live to see the day when there will be a Japanese man in the Council of the Twelve Apostles," Elder Brown said. "I do not know when it will be. I will not live to see it. Some of you young people will see it, and then you will realize that God loves the Japanese people, and you will join with other nations in forming a great and united Church all over the world. . . . I feel this in my heart tonight and I dare to make this prediction in the name of the Lord."[28]

In addition to this prediction, President Brown has made other predictions, including one where "documents record two occasions on which President Brown has told groups of missionaries that one among them, if he lives faithfully, 'will stand where I now stand as a member of the Council of the Twelve.'"[29] Also, "At a missionary meeting in Taipei [Taiwan], according to his journal, he 'was impressed to tell them that there was sitting in that room some young man who would one day stand in the Council of the Twelve, but before that day he would pass through the very fires of hell, but this great honor would come . . . if he lives worthy of it.'"[30]

Therefore, as President Heber J. Grant has stated, when one of the Apostles delivers a prophecy in the name of Jesus Christ it will be fulfilled. However, it is important to emphasize that the prediction or prophecy is conditioned on the man's worthiness and faithfulness.

THE TWELVE WILL NEVER INCREASE IN NUMBER

While it is true that there are fifteen ordained Apostles in the Church, there is only one Quorum of the Twelve Apostles. Three of the fifteen Apostles are usually members of the First Presidency. President David O. McKay of the First Presidency observed, "Some have asked whether the number twelve had any significance. Well, it has. The people to whom Jesus first came were the descendants of the twelve tribes of Israel. They were looking forward to an earthly king, as well as one who would stand at the head of these twelve tribes. Now it is not clearly stated anywhere in the scriptures whether Jesus chose the Twelve because there were twelve tribes of Israel, but the implication is that He did."[31]

President McKay also said:

> Now . . . I would hesitate about even mentioning this, associating the number twelve with the twelve tribes, but if you will turn to the Doctrine and Covenants, Section 29, verse 12, you will find the following:
>
> "Again, verily, verily, I say unto you, and it hath gone forth in a firm decree, by the will of the Father, that mine apostles, the Twelve which were with me in my ministry at Jerusalem, shall stand at my right hand at the day of my coming in a pillar of fire; being clothed with robes of righteousness, with crowns upon their heads, in glory even as I am, to judge the whole house of Israel, even as many as have loved me and kept my commandments, and none else."
>
> I think we need not pause longer on the significance of the number.[32]

In conjunction with those remarks, Elder Francis M. Lyman of the Twelve observed:

> The Apostles are not numerous and are not going to increase. . . . As the work spreads in Mexico and spreads in Canada, United States and elsewhere, as it is now doing, and new missions open up, the Apostles must go there, and to the Islands of the Sea. They must open up Japan and China, and if possible Russia, Austria, and other countries of Europe, and in all the world. . . . Whenever an Apostle is needed he will appear in any part of the earth, for . . . the apostles are to open the doors for missions and preside as leading Brethren in the Church. The hearts of the people should be open to receive them, and they should pray for them, for in their labors and ministering they are the Oracles of God, and speak words of instruction and words of wisdom.[33]

In reference to the Twelve Apostles never increasing in size, Elder Harold B. Lee said:

> In the early days of the Church, when it was horse and buggy days, they tell us that when the Stake Presidents would meet the brethren of the Church at the end of the railroad line, somewhere down in central Utah, and take them over the rough mountain roads to the next conference, a member of the Twelve, one of them particularly, would say, "Now my dear brethren remember we have hundreds of bishops and stake presidents, but only Twelve Apostles, so be careful." I have thought of that today, and some other days like today. The time is here when we will have to remember that there are only Twelve Apostles, and to stretch ourselves over the complete Church is no small task. It is almost getting to the time when, I am sure, that the time of the Twelve will be spent either in reorganizing or organizing new stakes somewhere throughout the world. We are almost to that today.[34]

The words spoken by these Apostles have literally come to pass. The Church has become a tremendous worldwide organization. Church membership continues to increase in size; however, the size of the Quorum of the Twelve Apostles will never increase. The number of members in that Quorum was established when the Lord lived on the earth and He personally called and ordained the Jewish Twelve.

A Special Witness

Let's focus our attention on the main reason each member of the Twelve was called to the Apostleship. We begin by using the words of President Harold B. Lee:

> I want to bear my testimony to you as one of those who has the responsibility to bear a special witness to the divine mission of the Lord. When we come into the Council of the Twelve, among other things, we are taken into an upper room in the [Salt Lake] temple, and there we are given what is called a "charge."
>
> Much of what is said is too sacred to repeat. But I

may say that my first responsibility is to bear witness of the divinity of the Lord and Savior, Jesus Christ. It is a humbling trust. A member of the Twelve is a special witness. My own witness came to me when I was assigned to give the talk on the Easter following the conference when I was sustained as a member of the Twelve. As I received the assignment, I was enjoined, "Now you understand that you are now to be a special witness of that great event, meaning the resurrection of the Lord." With that in mind, I closeted myself in one of the rooms of the Church Office Building. I read The Gospels carefully, particularly concerning the last days of the Master's life. I read of his crucifixion, his resurrection, and then his return for forty days following his resurrection, when he appeared to his disciples. Then I went to Nephi [in the Book of Mormon] and read about his appearance to the Nephites. As I read the story, I became aware that something was happening to me. It was not just the story I was reading. It seemed as though I was seeing. Those people were more real to me than I had ever known them before. I wondered if this was the more sure word of prophecy that I was experiencing. . . .

So I come to you with a witness as sure as was the Apostle Paul's. Perhaps in the manner in which the Apostle Paul received his. [Note these words:] A witness more perfect than sight is the witness which the Holy Ghost bears to one's soul so that he knows these things are true. I witness to you tonight with all my soul that I know, as the Spirit has born witness to my soul, that the Savior lives.[35]

Let's read what President Lee had to say about when he was first called as a counselor in the First Presidency of the Church:

On the day when I came to this call, which imposed a greater responsibility to be a witness of the mission of the Lord and Savior Jesus Christ—I suppose no one ever came to such a position without a lot of soul-searching, realizing his own inadequacy, and without the help of the Almighty—after a long night of searching and days of spiritual preparation that followed, I came to know as a witness more powerful than sight, until I could testify with a surety that defied all doubt, that I knew with every fiber of my soul that Jesus is the Christ, the Son of the Living God, that he lived, he died, he was resurrected, and today he presides in the heavens, directing the affairs of this church, which bears his name because it preaches his doctrine.[36]

In conjunction with these words, we turn to the expressions of Elder James A. Cullimore, assistant to the Twelve Apostles:

> The Twelve Apostles are special witnesses of the Savior. I don't know how many of them have actually seen a personage. They don't talk about it. But they don't have to, to receive their special witness that can come by the Holy Ghost.
>
> President Harold B. Lee said to a group of young people, "Not many have seen the Savior face to face here in mortality, but there is no one of you who has been blessed to receive the gift of the Holy Ghost after baptism but that may have a perfect assurance of his existence as though you had seen."[37]

In support of this teaching, we turn to the writings of President Joseph Fielding Smith, president of the Twelve:

> They [the Twelve] are special witness for Jesus Christ. It is their right to know the truth and to have an abiding witness. This is an exacting duty upon them, to know that Jesus Christ is in very deed the Only Begotten Son of God, the Redeemer of the world, and the Savior of all those who will confess their sins, repent, and keep his commandments.
>
> The question frequently arises: "Is it necessary for a member of the Council of the Twelve to see the Savior in order to be an Apostle?" It is their privilege to see him if occasion requires, but the Lord has taught that there is a stronger witness than seeing a personage, even seeing

the Son of God in a vision. Impressions on the soul that come from the Holy Ghost are far more significant than a vision. When Spirit speaks to spirit, the imprint upon the soul is far more difficult to erase. Every member of the Church should have impressions that Jesus is the Son of God indelibly pictured on his soul through the witness of the Holy Ghost.[38]

We can read accounts of various Apostles and prophets who have seen the Savior.[38] However, as has been explained by President Smith, there is a stronger witness than even seeing the Son of God in a vision—the witness of the Holy Ghost is far more significant!

In conclusion, consider the powerful words of Elder Mark E. Petersen, of the Twelve, who clearly explains why members of the Twelve are called to the apostleship:

> In the Council of the Twelve, men are bound together in a great brotherhood which can hardly be equaled anywhere else in the world. These men—these Twelve—have a special and distinctive calling from the Lord. They are chosen for one great purpose—to testify of Christ and teach his word. And this they do.
>
> One in their divine commission, one in a great effort to waken the world to its true opportunity to find peace and the abundant life, these men are united in heart and hand.
>
> They move as one. They work as one. They feel as one. . . .
>
> Like their associates in this great ministry, the Twelve know what it is to be devoted completely to the cause of Christ.
>
> Daily they go the extra mile. Daily they serve their Master with might and heart and soul, never counting the cost, willingly sacrificing even of their health and well-being as necessary, but always seeking to build the Kingdom of God with an eye single to his glory.[39]

TESTIMONY OF THE AUTHOR

It has been a privilege to research and write about the special men who are called to the apostleship in the only true and living Church—even

The Church of Jesus Christ of Latter-day Saints. I am thankful that the Brethren have spoken or written of their call. The Spirit has powerfully borne record that each Apostle is chosen by the Lord and revealed to the living prophet, who then ordains him. These chosen servants are called for one great purpose—to testify of Christ and teach His word. Our duty is to listen and heed their inspired teachings.

Notes

Preface

1. Bruce R. McConkie, *A New Witness for the Articles of Faith* (Salt Lake City: Deseret Book, 1985), 348–49.
2. *The Latter-day Saints' Millennial Star* 76 (26 February 1914), 131–32.
3. *Deseret News Semi-Weekly* 51, no. 15 (28 September 1895), 450.
4. Address, Regional Representative Seminar, 13 December 1969, 63.
5. Bruce R. McConkie, *The Mortal Messiah: From Bethlehem to Calvary,* 4 vols. (Salt Lake City: Deseret Book, 1980), 2:114.
6. *Deseret News 2001–2002 Church Almanac* (Salt Lake City: Deseret News 2002), 57.
7. Ibid., 68.
8. Joseph Smith, *History of The Church of Jesus Christ of Latter-day Saints,* ed. B. H. Roberts. 2d ed. rev., 7 vols. (Salt Lake City: The Church of Jesus Christ of Latter-day Saints, 1932–51), 1:267.
9. *Church Almanac,* 55.

Chapter 1

1. Bruce R. McConkie, *The Mortal Messiah: From Bethlehem to Calvary,* 4 vols. (Salt Lake City: Deseret Book, 1980), 2:100.
2. Ibid., 102–3.
3. James E. Talmage, *Jesus the Christ* (Salt Lake City: Deseret Book, 1962), 217–18; see also Matthew 10:1–4; Mark 3:13–19; Luke 6:12–16.
4. McConkie, 2:213 n. 2.
5. Talmage, n. 1, 521.
6. Alfred Edersheim, *The Life and Times of Jesus the Messiah,* rev. ed., 1896, vol. 2, 602.
7. McConkie, 4:223.

8. Talmage, 360.
9. Ibid., 361.
10. Ibid., 140.
11. Bruce R. McConkie, *Doctrinal New Testament Commentary,* 3 vols. (Salt Lake City: Bookcraft, 1965–73), 1:132.
12. Joseph Smith, *Teachings of the Prophet Joseph Smith,* sel. Joseph Fielding Smith (Salt Lake City: Deseret Book, 1938), 274.
13. McConkie, *The Mortal Messiah: From Bethlehem to Calvary,* 4 vols. (Salt Lake City: Deseret Book, 1979–81), 3:39.
14. Talmage, 376 n. 3.
15. Ibid., 370
16. Smith, *Teachings,* 158.
17. Bruce R. McConkie, *Mormon Doctrine,* 2d ed. (Salt Lake City: Bookcraft, 1966), 803.
18. McConkie, *The Mortal Messiah,* 3:57.
19. Talmage, 375.
20. McConkie, *The Mortal Messiah,* 3:57.
21. Ibid.
22. McConkie, *Doctrinal New Testament Commentary,* 1:401–2.
23. McConkie, *The Mortal Messiah,* 1:455.
24. Ibid., 3:92.
25. Talmage, 165
26. Ibid., 695.
27. Ibid., 700–01.
28. Joseph Fielding Smith, *Doctrines of Salvation,* comp. Bruce R. McConkie, 3 vols. (Salt Lake City: Bookcraft, 1954–56), 3:153.
29. Ibid., 3:152.
30. Ibid.
31. McConkie, *Doctrinal New Testament Commentary,* 2:182–84.
32. Ibid., 2:131.
33. Talmage, 717.
34. See D&C 27:12–13; see also Joseph Smith, *History of The Church of Jesus Christ of Latter-day Saints,* ed. B. H. Roberts, 2d ed. rev., 7 vols. (Salt Lake City: The Church of Jesus Christ of Latter-day Saints, 1932–51), 1:40–41.

Chapter 2

1. Sidney B. Sperry, *The Book of Mormon Testifies* (Salt Lake City: Bookcraft, 1952), 291; see also 3 Nephi 7:15–26.
2. Ibid., 306.
3. James E. Talmage, *Jesus the Christ* (Salt Lake City: Deseret Book, 1962), 744 n. 3.
4. Joseph Smith, *History of The Church of Jesus Christ of Latter-day Saints,* ed. B. H. Roberts, 2d ed. rev., 7 vols. (Salt Lake City: The Church of Jesus Christ of Latter-day Saints, 1932–51), 4:538.
5. Joseph Fielding Smith, *Answers to Gospel Questions,* 5 vols. (Salt Lake City: Deseret Book, 1957–66), 1:122.
6. Sperry, 305.
7. In *Journal of Discourses,* 26 vols. (London: Latter-day Saints' Book Depot, 1854–86), 24:191.

8. Smith, *Answers to Gospel Questions*, 3:39.
9. Ibid., 39–40.
10. Smith, *Answers to Gospel Questions*, 1:124.
11. Bruce R. McConkie, *The Mortal Messiah: From Bethlehem to Calvary*, 4 vols. (Salt Lake City: Deseret Book, 1981), 4:301.
12. Ibid., 301–2.
13. Bruce R. McConkie, *Our Leaders Speak—Eternal Truths Spoken at Brigham Young University*, sel. Soren F. Cox (Salt Lake City: Deseret Book, 1957), 137.
14. Talmage, 739–40.
15. Ibid.
16. Joseph Fielding Smith, *Doctrines of Salvation*, comp. Bruce R. McConkie, 3 vols. (Salt Lake City: Bookcraft, 1954–56), 3:232–34.
17. Smith, *Answers to Gospel Questions*, 1:122.

Chapter 3

1. Bruce R. McConkie, *A New Witness for the Articles of Faith* (Salt Lake City: Deseret Book, 1985), 5.
2. Joseph Fielding Smith, *Improvement Era* 38 (April 1935), 208–9; see also Joseph Fielding Smith, *Doctrines of Salvation*, comp. Bruce R McConkie, 3 vols. (Salt Lake City: Bookcraft, 1954–56), 3:146.
3. Wilford Woodruff, in *Journal of Discourses*, 26 vols. (London: Latter-day Saints' Book Depot, 1854–86), 4:147.
4. Smith, *Doctrines of Salvation*, 3:144–46.
5. McConkie, *A New Witness for the Articles of Faith*, 348–49.
6. James E. Talmage, *Millennial Star* 76 (26 February 1914), 131–32; approved by the First Presidency (see ibid., 136–37).
7. Spencer W. Kimball, *Faith Precedes the Miracle* (Salt Lake City: Deseret Book, 1972), 86, 88.
8. Smith, *Doctrines of Salvation*, 1:42–43.
9. Orson F. Whitney, in Conference Reports of The Church of Jesus Christ of Latter-day Saints (Salt Lake City: The Church of Jesus Christ of Latter-day Saints, 1898 to the present), October 1905, 93.
10. Orson F. Whitney, *Gospel Themes* (Salt Lake City: The Church of Jesus Christ of Latter-day Saints, 1913), 78–79.
11. Joseph F. Smith, *Personal Letterbooks*, 20 February 1881, 144, MS f 271, film reel 3, Book 2, LDS Church Archives.
12. Joseph Fielding Smith, letter to Neil H. Purdie, 3 January 1947, photocopy of the original letter in possession of the author.
13. Joseph Fielding Smith, *The Improvement Era* 38 (April 1935): 208–9; see also Smith, *Doctrines of Salvation*, 3:146.
14. Joseph Smith, *History of The Church of Jesus Christ of Latter-day Saints*, ed. B. H. Roberts, 2d ed. rev., 7 vols. (Salt Lake City: The Church of Jesus Christ of Latter-day Saints, 1932–51), 1:32–41; see also Joseph Fielding Smith, *Essentials in Church History*, 19th ed. (Salt Lake City: Deseret Book, 1964), 66–68.
15. Smith, *History of the Church*, 1:40–42; see also Smith, *Essentials in Church History*, 67–69.
16. Smith, *Doctrines of Salvation*, 3:147.

17. Joseph F. Smith, letter to Joseph Fielding Smith, *Personal Letterbook*, 12 November 1900, 403–4, Ms. F, 271, film reel 8.
18. Smith, *Doctrines of Salvation*, 3:147.
19. Brigham Young, in Matthias F. Cowley, *Wilford Woodruff—History of His Life and Labors* (Salt Lake City: Deseret News Press, 1909), 319–20; see also *Journal of Discourses,* 1:137; 9:87, 281.
20. McConkie, *A New Witness for the Articles of Faith*, 321–22.
21. Smith, *Doctrines of Salvation*, 3:147–48; see also Smith, *History of the Church,* 1:40–41, 76–78.
22. Ibid., 3:144–49; see also Bruce R. McConkie, *Mormon Doctrine*, 2d ed. (Salt Lake City: Bookcraft, 1966), 47.
23. See Smith, *History of the Church,* 1:40–42.
24. Ibid., 1:40–42, nn.
25. Ibid., 1:40–41, 74–79.
26. Ibid., 1:175–76; see also Smith, *Essentials in Church History,* 126; *Journal of Discourses,* 9:89.
27. See Smith, *History of the Church,* 1:267.

Chapter 4

1. Brigham Young, in *Journal of Discourses*, 26 vols. (London: Latter-day Saints' Book Depot, 1854–86), 9:89.
2. Joseph Young Sr., *History of the Organization of the Seventies* (Salt Lake City: Deseret News Steam Printing Establishment, 1878), 1–2; see also Joseph Smith, *History of The Church of Jesus Christ of Latter-day Saints*, ed. B. H. Roberts, 2d ed. rev., 7 vols. (Salt Lake City: The Church of Jesus Christ of Latter-day Saints, 1932–51), 2:181 nn.
3. D&C 81; 90:6, 19; see also Smith, *History of the Church,* 1:334.
4. McLellin is spelled "M'Lellin" in the *History of the Church,* 1:187. However, Elder Joseph Fielding Smith spells it McLellin in *Doctrines of Salvation*, comp. Bruce R. McConkie, 3 vols. (Salt Lake City: Bookcraft, 1954–56), 3:150. It appears here as McLellin for easier pronunciation.
5. Smith, *History of the Church,* 2:180–87; see also Smith, *Doctrines of Salvation*, 3:149–50.
6. Ibid., 1:2.
7. Smith, *Doctrines of Salvation*, 3:150; for further information on the ordination of the Twelve by the Three Witnesses, see Smith, *History of the Church,* 2:187–94 nn.
8. *Times and Seasons* 11:868; see also Smith, *History of the Church,* 2:188 nn.
9. Smith, *History of the Church,* 2:219; see also Smith, *Doctrines of Salvation*, 3:150; Joseph Fielding Smith, *Essentials in Church History,* 19th ed. (Salt Lake City: Deseret Book, 1964), 181, 692–94.
10. Joseph F. Smith, *Improvement Era* 5 (May 1902): 549; see also Joseph F. Smith, *Gospel Doctrine* (Salt Lake City: Deseret Book, 1973), 175.
11. Smith, History of the Church, 2:194–98.
12. Ibid., 2:198, n.
13. William E. McLellin, *Council of Twelve Minutes*, 27 February 1834, Kirtland, Ohio, LDS Church Archives; a similar version is recorded in Smith, *History of the Church,* 2:198–200.

14. Smith, *History of the Church,* 2:200.
15. Joseph Anderson, devotional address, 1 March 1975, 4.
16. Smith, *History of the Church,* 2:209–17, 222; see also Smith, *Essentials in Church History,* 183.
17. Smith, *History of the Church,* 2:243–45; see also Smith, *Essentials in Church History,* 184–86.
18. Smith, *Doctrines of Salvation,* 3:150–51.

Chapter 5

1. Joseph Smith, *History of The Church of Jesus Christ of Latter-day Saints,* ed. B. H. Roberts, 2d ed. rev., 7 vols. (Salt Lake City: The Church of Jesus Christ of Latter-day Saints, 1932–51), 2:287; Joseph Fielding Smith, *Essentials in Church History,* 19th ed. (Salt Lake City: Deseret Book, 1964), 186.
2. Smith, *History of the Church,* 2:300–301.
3. Ibid., 302.
4. Ibid., 307–10.
5. Ibid., 378–81; Smith, *Essentials in Church History,* 188.
6. Orson F. Whitney, *Life of Heber C. Kimball,* 1st ed. (Salt Lake City, 1888), 105–6.
7. Smith, *History of the Church,* 2:381.
8. Ibid., 382–83.
9. *Minutes of the School of the Prophets,* held at Provo, Utah, 18 May 1868 (L. Tom Perry Special Collections, Harold B. Lee Library, Brigham Young University); in *Journal of Discourses,* 26 vols. (London: Latter-day Saints' Book Depot, 1854–86), 9:376.
10. President Heber C. Kimball, first counselor to President Brigham Young, an address delivered in the tabernacle, at Salt Lake City, Utah, on 9 February 1862, as recorded in the *Journal of Discourses,* 9:376.
11. *Minutes of the School of the Prophets,* Provo, Utah, 18 May 1868 (L. Tom Perry Special Collections, Harold B. Lee Library, Brigham Young University); in *Journal of Discourses,* 26 vols. (London: Latter-day Saints' Book Depot, 1854–86), 9:376.
12. Smith, *History of the Church,* 2:410–17.
13. Joseph Fielding Smith, *Doctrines of Salvation,* comp. Bruce R. McConkie, 3 vols. (Salt Lake City: Bookcraft, 1954–56), 2:240; see also Smith, *History of the Church,* 2:410–28.
14. Smith, *History of the Church,* 1:322–24.
15. Smith, *History of the Church,* 2:287.
16. Ibid., 2:308–9.
17. Ibid., 2:430–31.
18. Bruce R. McConkie, *Mormon Doctrine,* 2d ed. (Salt Lake City: Bookcraft, 1966), 831.
19. Smith, *Doctrines of Salvation,* 2:241–42.
20. Smith, *History of the Church,* 2:431.

Chapter 6

1. Joseph Smith, *History of The Church of Jesus Christ of Latter-day Saints,* ed. B. H. Roberts, 2d ed. rev., 7 vols. (Salt Lake City: The Church of Jesus Christ of Latter-day Saints, 1932–51), 2:219.

2. Ibid., 2:219, n.
3. Ibid., 2:220.
4. *Millennial Star* 43 (2 May 1881): 278; conference address given 4 April 1881.
5. George A. Smith, in *Journal of Discourses,* 26 vols. (London: Latter-day Saints' Book Depot, 1854–86), 3:283.
6. Ibid., 3:284.
7. Smith, *History of the Church,* 3:283–84 (minutes of the conference at Quincy, Illinois).
8. Joseph Fielding Smith, *Essentials in Church History,* 19th ed. (Salt Lake City: Deseret Book, 1964), 693.
9. See Bruce E. Dana, *The Three Nephites and Other Translated Beings* (Springville, Utah: Bonneville Books, 2003), 99–109; see also Lycurgus A. Wilson, *The Life of David W. Patten* (*The Deseret News,* 1900; reprint, Grantsville, Utah: Archive Publishers, 2000), 45–47.
10. Smith, *History of the Church,* 3:171.
11. Brigham Young, in *Journal of Discourses,* 13:216; discourse given in the Tabernacle, Salt Lake City, 17 July 1870.
12. Ibid., 3:51; discourse given in the Bowery, Salt Lake City, 6 October, 1855.
13. Smith, *History of the Church,* 4:115–16, n.; see also ibid., 2:187, 219–20.
14. Ibid., 7:623.
15. Journal Entry, *The Instructor* 80 (June 1945): 258–59.
16. Orson F. Whitney, *Life of Heber C. Kimball,* 2d ed. (Salt Lake City, Bookcraft, 1945), 105, 241–42.
17. Smith, *History of the Church,* 7:623.
18. Smith, *Essentials in Church History,* 540.
19. Smith, *History of the Church,* 3:166–67; see also Smith, *Essentials in Church History,* 225–27.
20. Ibid., 3:379; see also Smith, *Essentials in Church History,* 227.
21. Smith, *Essentials in Church History,* 201.
22. Ibid., 227, 284.
23. Smith, *History of the Church* 1:226; see also Smith, *Essentials in Church History,* 140–41.
24. Smith, *History of the Church,* 3:31.
25. Ibid., 3:31, n.; see also Smith, *Essentials in Church History,* 693.
26. Parley P. Pratt, *Autobiography of Parley P. Pratt,* ed. Parley P. Pratt Jr., 1st ed. (New York: 1874), 183–84; B. H. Roberts, *Life of John Taylor,* 1st ed. (1892; reprint, Salt Lake City: Bookcraft, 1963), 39–41; see also Smith, *History of the Church,* 2:488–89.
27. Smith, *Essentials in Church History,* 492–93, 693.
28. Smith, *History of the Church,* 2:528; see also Smith, *Essentials in Church History,* 200.
29. Smith, *Essentials in Church History,* 693–94.
30. Ibid., 694.
31. Andrew Jenson, *L.D.S. Biographical Encyclopedia,* 4 vols. (Andrew Jenson History Company, 1901; reprint, Salt Lake City: Deseret Press, 1901–1936), 1:86.
32. Smith, *History of the Church,* 2:295–97.
33. Ibid., 2:334–35.
34. Smith, *Essentials in Church History,* 694; other sources say 19 October 1845 (see *Deseret News 2001–2002 Church Almanac* (Salt Lake City: *Deseret News,* 2002), 63.

NOTES

35. Smith, History of the Church, 7:457–59, 483.
36. Smith, *Essentials in Church* History, 332; see also Smith, *History of the Church,* 5:120.
37. Smith, *History of the Church,* 5:252.
38. Ibid., 2:253–56; see also 7:236 n.
39. Brigham Young, in *Journal of Discourses,* 16:10.
40. Brigham Young Secretary's Journal, 1 October 1860, LDS Church Archives; Leonard J. Arrington, *Brigham Young: American Moses* (Urbana, Ill.: University of Illinois Press., 1986), 208.
41. In Conference Reports of The Church of Jesus Christ of Latter-day Saints (Salt Lake City: The Church of Jesus Christ of Latter-day Saints, 1898 to present), October 1925, 174.
42. Smith, *History of the Church,* 2:528; see also Smith, *Essentials in Church History,* 200.
43. Smith, *Essentials in Church History,* 694; the *Church Almanac,* page 64, says the year was 1837.
44. Smith, *History of the Church,* 4:115–16 n.; see also 2:187, 219–20.
45. Ibid., 2:528; see also Smith, *Essentials in Church History,* 200.
46. Ibid., 3:20; see also Smith, *Essentials in Church History,* 694.
47. Smith, *Essentials in Church History,* 364–65.
48. Ezra Taft Benson, in Conference Report, October 1963, 15.
49. Smith, *History of the Church,* 3:46–47.
50. Ibid., 3:240–41 (Minutes of the High Council at Far West).
51. Ibid., 4:372; see also Smith, *Essentials in Church History,* 284.
52. Ibid., 7:582.
53. Smith, *Essentials in Church History,* 694.
54. Smith, *History of the Church,* 3:240–41; see also Smith, *Essentials in Church History,* 694.
55. Ibid., 6:614–19; see also D&C 135; Smith, *Essentials in Church History,* 382–84.
56. Ibid., 6:629–31.
57. Smith, *Essentials in Church History,* 576.
58. Ibid., 686.
59. Smith, *History of the Church,* 3:336–37.
60. Smith, *Essentials in Church History,* 686.
61. Boyd K. Packer, *The Holy Temple* (Salt Lake City: Bookcraft, 1980), 189.
62. Official Declaration—1, as recorded in *Doctrine and Covenants,* 291–93.
63. Smith, *Essentials in Church History,* 609–10.
64. Ibid., 614.
65. Smith, *History of the Church,* 3:336–38, 345.
66. Smith, *Essentials in Church History,* 277, 279, 401, 451, 491, 540, 695.
67. Smith, *History of the Church,* 4:114; see also Brigham Young letter, 4:115.
68. Ibid., 4:463, 540–41, 695.
69. Ibid., 4:341.
70. Ibid., 4:340–41.
71. Smith, *Essentials in Church History,* 695.
72. Smith, *History of the Church,* 5:119–20; see also Smith, *Essentials in Church History,* 463.
73. Ibid., 5:255–56.
74. Ibid., 7: 236 n.; see also 7:248.
75. Amasa Lyman, in *Journal of Discourses,* 3:220.
76. Smith, *Essentials in Church History,* 539, 695.

Chapter 7

1. D&C 27:12–13; 128:20–21.
2. See chapter 3.
3. Joseph Smith, *History of The Church of Jesus Christ of Latter-day Saints,* ed. B. H. Roberts, 2d ed. rev., 7 vols. (Salt Lake City: The Church of Jesus Christ of Latter-day Saints, 1932–51), 1:267.
4. Ibid., 1:334.
5. Ibid., 2:209–10, 222.
6. Ibid., 2:210–17.
7. Ibid., 2:374.
8. Joseph Fielding Smith, *Improvement Era,* November 1956, 788.
9. Wilford Woodruff, from an address delivered 19 March 1897, in *Official Report of the First British Area General Conference of The Church of Jesus Christ of Latter-day Saints,* Manchester, England, 27 August 1897 (Salt Lake City: The Church of Jesus Christ of Latter-day Saints, 1897), 42.
10. Wilford Woodruff, from an address delivered 29 August 1897, in *Deseret News Weekly* 55, no. 12 (4 September 1897): 356.
11. *Times and Seasons* 5:651; see also Joseph Fielding Smith, *Doctrines of Salvation,* comp. Bruce R. McConkie, 3 vols. (Salt Lake City: Bookcraft, 1954–56), 3:154.
12. Smith, *History of the Church,* 1:334; see also *History of the Church* 4:229 n., 286 n.; D&C 124:91–96; Lucy Mack Smith, *History of Joseph Smith, by His Mother* (Salt Lake City: Bookcraft, 1958), 334.
13. D&C 135; see also Smith, *History of the Church,* 6:617–18, 629–31.
14. Joseph Fielding Smith, *Essentials in Church History,* 19th ed. (Salt Lake City: Deseret Book, 1964), 385.
15. Brigham Young, from an address delivered 25 December 1857, Ms d 1234, box 49, folder 3; and Ms f 219, reel #82, 4, typescript, LDS Church Archives.
16. Smith, *History of the Church,* 7:223–30; see also Smith, *Essentials in Church History,* 385–87.
17. The Private Journal of William Hyde, 13–15; copy of journal in possession of author.
18. Smith, *Essentials in Church History,* 388.
19. Ibid., 389.
20. Smith, *History of the Church,* 7:236–42; see also Smith, *Essentials in Church History,* 388–89.
21. Smith, *Essentials in Church History,* 389.
22. Remarks given at the Mill Creek Ward, in Salt Lake City, on 7 May 1861, as recorded in *Journal of Discourses,* 9:87; see also in *Journal of Discourses,* 1:137; 9:281.
23. An address given 8 July 1900; published in *Deseret News Semi-Weekly,* no. 42 (20 July 1900): 10.
24. George Q. Cannon, from an address given 8 July 1900, in *Deseret News Semi-Weekly* 42 (20 July 1900), 10.
25. Spencer W. Kimball, "We Thank Thee, O God, for a Prophet," *Ensign,* January 1973, 34.
26. In Gordon B. Hinckley, "This Work Is Concerned with People," *Ensign,* May 1995, 51.

27. Spencer W. Kimball, from an address delivered to missionaries in California, 2 January 1959, 17–18.
28. *Korea Conference Report*, 17 August 1975, 39.
29. N. Eldon Tanner, *Administration of the Restored Church*, Brigham Young University Speeches of the Year (8 January 1978), 203.

Chapter 8

1. Joseph Smith, *History of The Church of Jesus Christ of Latter-day Saints,* ed. B. H. Roberts, 2d ed. rev., 7 vols. (Salt Lake City: The Church of Jesus Christ of Latter-day Saints, 1932–51), 7:240; see also Joseph Fielding Smith, *Essentials in Church History*, 19th ed. (Salt Lake City: Deseret Book, 1964), 389.
2. Smith, *Essentials in Church History,* 389.
3. *The Juvenile Instructor* 14 (1 June 1879): 128; a similar description by George Q. Cannon appeared in *The Juvenile Instructor* 6 (23 December 1871): 203.
4. Emerson Roy West, *Latter-day Prophets: Their Lives, Teachings, and Testimonies, with Profiles of Their Wives* (American Fork, Utah: Covenant Communications, 1997), 30. Concerning Wilford Woodruff's statement, Brother West quotes Susan McCloud, *Brigham Young: A Personal Portrait* (American Fork, Utah: Covenant Communications, 1997), 244.
5. Joseph F. Smith, *Gospel Doctrine: Selections from the Sermons and Writings of Joseph F. Smith* (Salt Lake City: Deseret Book, 1973), 172.
6. *Deseret News 2001–2002 Church Almanac* (Salt Lake City: *Deseret News,* 2002), 54.
7. Smith, *History of the Church,* 7:621, 623.
8. See also ibid., 7:621 n.
9. D&C 81; 90:6, 19; see also Smith, *History of the Church,* 1:334.
10. Joseph Fielding Smith, *Doctrines of Salvation,* comp. Bruce R. McConkie, 3 vols. (Salt Lake City: Bookcraft, 1954–56), 3:150; for further information on the ordination of the Twelve by the Three Witnesses, see Smith, *History of the Church,* 2:187–94 nn.
11. Smith, *Essentials in Church History,* 388–89.
12. *Wilford Woodruff's Journal,* Wilford Woodruff Papers, LDS Church Archives, 23 August 1862; see also Smith, *History of the Church* 7:621.
13. Ibid.
14. George Q. Cannon, from an address given 8 July 1900, in *Deseret News Semi-Weekly* 42 (20 July 1900): 10.
15. Heber C. Kimball, from an address given 25 August 1865, in the *Deseret News* 14, no. 48 (30 August 1865): 377.
16. Brigham Young, in *Journal of Discourses,* 26 vols. (London: Latter-day Saints' Book Depot, 1854–86), 6:320.
17. George Q. Cannon, in *Journal of Discourses* 19:233–34.
18. *2001–2002 Church Almanac,* 54.
19. Smith, *History of the Church,* 3:240–41; see also Smith, *Essentials in Church History,* 694.
20. *Wilford Woodruff Journal,* revelation given 26 January 1880.

21. Ibid.
22. George Q. Cannon, in *Journal of Discourses,* 23:365.
23. Smith, *Essentials in Church History,* 589.
24. Ibid., 694.
25. Letter written 7 August 1887, Salt Lake City.
26. Smith, *History of the Church,* 3:336–37.
27. Ibid., 694.
28. Ibid., 603.
29. General conference address, 6 October 1890, printed in *Millennial Star* 52 (24 November 1890): 737–38.
30. L. John Nuttall, *His Daily Journal,* 5 April 1889, 386–89, LDS Church Archives. Brother Nuttall was president of the Kanab Stake from 1877 to 1884. In addition, he was called in 1879 to be the private secretary of President John Taylor. After serving President Taylor for eight years, Brother Nuttall, who kept a detailed journal, then served as private secretary to President Wilford Woodruff until 1992.
31. Smith, *Essentials in Church History,* 615.
32. Calculations are based on each year having 365 days. See Smith, *Essentials in Church History,* 623, 638, 654, 661; Spencer W. Kimball, *Faith Precedes the Miracle* (Salt Lake City: Deseret Book, 1979), 315–16.

Chapter 9

1. Brigham Young, in *Journal of Discourses,* 26 vols. (London: Latter-day Saints' Book Depot, 1854–86), 6:320 (discourse given 7 April 1852).
2. Joseph F. Smith, *Gospel Doctrine,* 1st ed. (Salt Lake City: *Deseret News,* 1919), 216; and 7th ed. (Salt Lake City: Deseret Book, 1946), 173.
3. Joseph F. Smith, *Improvement Era,* 5 (May 1902), 549; see also Smith, *Gospel Doctrine,* 7th ed., 173–74.
4. Joseph F. Smith, *Essentials in Church History,* 19th ed. (Salt Lake City: Deseret Book, 1964), 307–8.
5. Joseph Fielding Smith, *Doctrines of Salvation,* comp. Bruce R. McConkie, 3 vols. (Salt Lake City: Bookcraft, 1954–56), 3:147.
6. John Taylor and George A. Smith, *Historians Private Journal,* Ms f 348, #4, 25, LDS Church Archives.
7. Ibid.
8. *Deseret News 2001–2002 Church Almanac* (Salt Lake City: *Deseret News,* 2002), 57, 61, 69. Concerning Brigham Young Jr., see also Smith, *Essentials in Church History,* 540. Regarding John W. Young, see *Essentials in Church History,* 688.
9. *Church Almanac,* 54.
10. Smith, *Essentials in Church History,* 539.
11. Ibid., 623, 686.
12. Ibid., 696.
13. Ibid., 690.
14. *Church Almanac,* 57.
15. In *Millennial Star* 52 (19 May 1890): 308.
16. Personal correspondence from Ronald W. Read, reference librarian, Family and Church History Department, 20 October 2004.

17. Reed C. Durham Jr. and Steven H. Heath, *Succession in the Church* (Salt Lake City: Bookcraft, 1970), 88.
18. *Church Almanac*, 57.
19. In Conference Reports of The Church of Jesus Christ of Latter-day Saints. Salt Lake City: The Church of Jesus Christ of Latter-day Saints, 1898 to present), April 1938, 95.
20. David O. McKay, *Relief Society Magazine* 25 (December 1938): 812.
21. Smith, *Essentials in Church History*, 523, 612, 596–97.
22. In Conference Report, 29 September 1967, 1–2, 25, 40.
23. Ibid., 40–41.
24. *Church Almanac*, 62.

Chapter 10

1. Matthias F. Cowley, *Wilford Woodruff, History of His Life and Labors* [Salt Lake City: Bookcraft, 1964), 93.
2. Joseph Fielding Smith, *Essentials in Church History*, 19th ed. (Salt Lake City: Deseret Book, 1964), 214, 262, 603–14, 695.
3. *Journal of George A. Smith,* 1817–1852, Ms d 1322, box 4, LDS Church Archives.
4. Smith, *Essentials in Church History*, 695.
5. *Life of Franklin D. Richards* (1924), 81–82; journal entry, 13 August 1847.
6. Lorenzo Snow, *Deseret News Semi-Weekly* 34, no. 85 (19 December 1899): 5.
7. Smith, *Essentials in Church History*, 696.
8. Joseph J. Cannon, *The Instructor* 79 (December 1944): 577–78.
9. George Q. Cannon, *Deseret News Weekly* 40, no. 12 (15 March 1890): 377; see *Millennial Star* 52 (24 November 1890): 738 for a similar conference address.
10. George Q. Cannon, *Deseret News Weekly* 54, no 22 (15 May 1897): 676.
11. *Journal Entry*, 8 October 1880; in Joseph J. Cannon, *The Instructor* 80 (September 1945): 410–11.
12. Smith, *Essentials in Church History*, 589, 603, 696.
13. Cowley, *Wilford Woodruff,* 445–46.
14. Joseph Fielding Smith, *Life of Joseph F. Smith* (Salt Lake City: Deseret Book, 1938) 226–28.
15. Ibid.
16. Ibid., 535–36.
17. In Conference Report, 1 June 1919, 10–11.
18. *Essentials in Church History*, 623–37.
19. Heber J. Grant, in Conference Reports of The Church of Jesus Christ of Latter-day Saints (Salt Lake City: The Church of Jesus Christ of Latter-day Saints, 1898 to present), April 1935, 13–14; see also *Millennial Star* 84:18, for same experience.
20. Heber J. Grant, *Millennial Star* 84 (5 January 1922): 5–6.
21. Heber J. Grant, in Conference Report, October 1941, 12.
22. Ibid., October 1919, 123–25; see also *Young Women's Journal* 11:55.
23. Ibid., October 1942, 24; emphasis added.
24. Ibid., 24–25.
25. Smith, *Essentials in Church History*, 590.
26. Dated 22 October 1882, as recorded in *Improvement Era* 41 (November 1938): 650.

27. Ibid.
28. *The Instructor* 74 (January 1939), 4.
29. Smith, *Essentials in Church History*, 589–90, 697.
30. Ibid., 589, 638–53, 697.
31. "Brief Remarks," *Millennial Star* 51 (2 December 1889): 753–54.
32. *His Daily Journal*, 126–27, 6 October 1889, LDS Church Archives.
33. Ibid., 130, 7 October 1889.
34. Smith, *Essentials in Church History*, 697–98.
35. *Improvement Era* 2 (February 1899): 263.
36. Andrew Jenson, *L.D.S. Biographical Encyclopedia*, 4 vols. (Andrew Jenson History Company, 1901; reprint, Salt Lake City: Deseret Press, 1901–1936), 1:154.
37. Smith, *Essentials in Church History*, 630.
38. Ibid., 631.
39. Spencer W. Kimball, *The Miracle of Forgiveness* (Salt Lake City: Bookcraft, 1969), 298.
40. Smith, *Essentials in Church History*, 698; *Deseret News 2001–2002 Church Almanac* (Salt Lake City: *Deseret News*, 2002), 66.
41. Address by president of the Twelve, 13 March 1927, "Seventieth Birthday Celebration," Rudger Clawson Collection, Ms. 581, Bx 6, Marriott Library, University of Utah.
42. Ibid.
43. Ibid.
44. Smith, *Essentials in Church History*, 698.
45. Arthur R. Bassett, *New Era*, January 1972, 4.
46. Excerpts from "Diary—George Albert Smith Papers," Ms 36, box 14, folder 1, 1, University of Utah Library.
47. George Albert Smith, in Conference Report, April 1949, 84–85.
48. Smith, *Essentials in Church History*, 654–60, 698.
49. *Millennial Star* 74 (10 October 1912): 642.
50. Smith, *Essentials in Church History*, 698–99.
51. Orson F. Whitney, *Through Memory's Halls* (Salt Lake City: Deseret News Press, 1930), 191–92.
52. Smith, *Essentials in Church History*, 616.
53. Whitney, *Through Memory's Halls*, 191–92.
54. Ibid., 113.
55. Ibid., 182.
56. Smith, *Essentials in Church History*, 699.
57. David O. McKay, in Conference Report, October 1968, 86.
58. Smith, *Essentials in Church History*, 661–85, 699.
59. The Journal of Anthony W. Ivins, LDS Church Archives, 11 December 1895.
60. In Conference Report, April 1934, 16.
61. Photocopy of original letter in possession of the author, 7–8, LDS Church Archives.
62. The Journal of Anthony W. Ivins, 7 October 1907, LDS Church Archives.
63. Smith, *Essentials in Church History*, 641–42, 699.
64. D. Arthur Haycock, *Exemplary Manhood Award*, Brigham Young University Speeches of the Year, 18 April 1972, 3.
65. Bruce R. McConkie, *Ensign*, August 1972, 29–30.
66. Joseph F. McConkie, *True and Faithful: The Life Story of Joseph Fielding Smith* (Salt Lake City: Bookcraft, 1971), 35.

67. *Prophets I have known*, 1973, 171.
68. Smith, *Essentials in Church History*, 699.
69. Heber J. Grant, in Conference Report, April 1941, 6; see also Spencer W. Kimball, *Faith Precedes the Miracle* (Salt Lake City: Deseret Book, 1979), 39.
70. Kimball, *Faith Precedes the Miracle*, 43.
71. Smith, *Essentials in Church History*, 700.
72. *The Instructor* 72 (February 1937): 54, 56.
73. Joseph Fielding Smith, "Patriarchal Blessings," an address given 15 June 1956, 7.
74. Smith, *Essentials in Church History*, 700.
75. *Church News*, 5 January 1974, 16.
76. Russell M. Nelson, *From Heart to Heart: An Autobiography* (Salt Lake City: Russell Marion Nelson, 1979), 164–65.
77. Smith, *Essentials in Church History*, 701; *Deseret News 2001–2002 Church Almanac* (Salt Lake City: *Deseret News*, 2002), 56.
78. Ezra Taft Benson, "The Image of a General Authority," an address given 19 January 1977, 1.
79. Smith, *Essentials in Church History*, 701; *Deseret News 2001–2002 Church Almanac* (Salt Lake City: *Deseret News*, 2002), 56.
80. Matthew Cowley, *Miracles*, Brigham Young University Speeches of the Year, 18 February 1953, 7.
81. Smith, *Essentials in Church History*, 701; *Deseret News 2001–2002 Church Almanac* (Salt Lake City: *Deseret News*, 2002), 68.
82. Henry D. Moyle, seminary and institute address, Salt Lake City, 27 June 1962, 6–7.
83. Henry D. Moyle, *New England Mission Monthly Bulletin* 2, no. 2 (February 1962); address delivered in Geneva, Switzerland, 30 October 1961.
84. Smith, *Essentials in Church History*, 701.
85. Delbert L. Stapley, in Conference Report, October 1950, 97.
86. Ibid.
87. Smith, *Essentials in Church History*, 701;
88. Stapley, in Conference Report, October 1951, 124.
89. Smith, *Essentials in Church History*, 701–2.
90. Eugene E. Campbell and Richard D. Poll, *Hugh B. Brown His Life and Thought* (Salt Lake City: Bookcraft, 1975), 37, 220–21.
91. Hugh B. Brown, *The Abundant Life—The Memoirs of Hugh B. Brown* (Salt Lake City: Bookcraft, 1979), 126–27.
92. Smith, *Essentials in Church History*, 702.
93. Sheri L. Dew, *Go Forward with Faith, The Biography of Gordon B. Hinckley* (Salt Lake City: Deseret Book, 1996), 60, 234.
94. Ibid.
95. Smith, *Essentials in Church History*, 702.

Chapter 11

1. Joseph Smith, *History of The Church of Jesus Christ of Latter-day Saints,* ed. H. Roberts, 2d ed. rev., 7 vols. (Salt Lake City: The Church of Jesus Christ of Latter-day Saints, 1932–51), 1:76; see also Joseph Fielding Smith, *Essentials in Church History,* 19th ed. (Salt Lake City: Deseret Book, 1964), 91.

2. *Deseret News 2001–2002 Church Almanac* (Salt Lake City: *Deseret News,* 2002), 584.
3. Ibid.
4. J. Reuben Clark, in Conference Reports of The Church of Jesus Christ of Latter-day Saints (Salt Lake City: The Church of Jesus Christ of Latter-day Saints, 1898 to present), April 1941, 94.
5. Letter from Family and Church History Department, Salt Lake City, 20 October 2004.
6. J. Reuben Clark, in Conference Report, April 1941, 94–95.
7. "Melchizedek Priesthood, Assistants to the Twelve," *Improvement Era,* October 1956, 752.
8. An Address, *Regional Welfare Meeting,* 21 January 1960, 1–2.
9. "Melchizedek Priesthood, Assistants to the Twelve," 752.
10. *Church Almanac,* 75–77.
11. Lucile C. Tate, *Boyd K. Packer: A Watchman on the Tower* (Salt Lake City: Bookcraft, 1995), 235.
12. Ibid., 236.
13. Ibid., 237.
14. Ibid., 238.
15. Gordon B. Hinckley, "This Work Is Concerned with People," *Ensign,* May 1995, 51.
16. *Deseret News* 1999–2000 *Church Almanac* (Salt Lake City: *Deseret News,* 2000), 144.
17. Hinckley, "This Work Is Concerned with People," 51.

Chapter 12

1. Harold B. Lee, in Conference Reports of The Church of Jesus Christ of Latter-day Saints (Salt Lake City: The Church of Jesus Christ of Latter-day Saints, 1898 to present), April 1963, 88.
2. Ibid., October 1969, 60.
3. General conference address, 3 April 1892, in *Millennial Star* 54 (9 May 1892), 290.
4. Joseph F. Smith, *Gospel Doctrine: Selections from the Sermons and Writings of Joseph F. Smith* (Salt Lake City: Deseret Book, 1973), 155.
5. Brigham Young, in *Journal of Discourses,* 8:55.
6. *The Contributor* 17 (April 1896), 354.
7. In Conference Report, 8 April 1950, 101.
8. Ibid., in Conference Report, April 1950, 101.
9. Harold B. Lee, *Joseph Smith—His Mission Divine,* 131.
10. Richard L. Evans, *Improvement Era,* October 1954, 746.
11. Boyd K. Packer, *Ensign,* March 1974, 5.
12. "Eternal Progress," address at the Church College of Hawaii, 16 October 1964, 8–10; a similar address by Elder Hugh B. Brown, "Eternal Values Night," was given at Ricks College, 20 February 1968, 10–11; see also Leon Hartshorn, *Outstanding Stories by General Authorities,* 16–18.
13. *Church News,* 15 July 1972, 6; President Tanner related this experience on 3 October 1969 in an address titled "A Meeting with the Patriarchs," 3–4.
14. *Deseret News Weekly* 29, no. 34 (22 September 1880): 536.

15. Boyd K. Packer, "The Mantle Is Far, Far Greater than the Intellect," address delivered 22 August 1981; see Boyd K. Packer, *Let Your Heart Not Be Troubled* (Salt Lake City: Bookcraft, 1991), 106–8.
16. Ezra Taft Benson, in Conference Report, April 1974, 151.
17. James E. Faust, "Where Do I Make My Stand?" *Ensign*, November 2004, 18.
18. Spencer W. Kimball, address delivered to missionaries in California, 2 January 1959, 16. He delivered similar remarks to a Berlin mission conference, 15 January 1962, 1–2.
19. N. Eldon Tanner, *Administration of the Restored Church*, Brigham Young University Speeches of the Year (8 January 1978), 209.
20. Spencer W. Kimball, address delivered to missionaries in California, 2 January 1959, 6.
21. *Deseret News Semi-Weekly*, 20 July 1900; see also *Millennial Star* 62 (9 August 1900), 499.
22. Ezra Taft Benson, "The Image of a General Authority," address delivered 19 January 1977, 1.
23. Spencer W. Kimball, *Circles of Exaltation,* Brigham Young University Speeches of the Year, 28 June 1968, 6.
24. Lucile C. Tate, *Boyd K. Packer: A Watchman on the Tower* (Salt Lake City: Bookcraft, 1995), 182.
25. Heber J. Grant, *Improvement Era* 40 (December 1937), 735.
26. Eugene E. Campbell and Richard D. Poll, *Hugh B. Brown: His Life and Thought* (Salt Lake City: Bookcraft, 1975), 147–48.
27. Ibid., 272; prediction made about the year 1967.
28. Ibid., 222.
29. Ibid., 272.
30. David O. McKay, *Relief Society Magazine* 25 (December 1938); 806–7; from an address delivered 4 October 1938.
31. Ibid.
32. Francis M. Lyman, address delivered 6 June 1896, Ms d 1261, Box 2, folder 14, 5, LDS Church Archives.
33. Harold B. Lee, address delivered prior to dedicating South Bountiful Third and Fourth Wards, no date, 1.
34. Harold B. Lee, *Laurels,* Brigham Young University Speeches of the Year, 27 September 1971, 30–31.
35. British Area Conference Report, 29 August 1971, 142.
36. James Cullimore, in Conference Report, April 1972, 46.
37. Joseph Fielding Smith, *Improvement Era*, November 1966, 979.
38. See Bruce E. Dana, *The Eternal Father and His Son* (Springville, Utah: Cedar Fort, 2004), 123–43.
39. Mark E. Petersen, "Funeral for Richard L. Evans, of the Twelve," address delivered 4 November 1971, 1.

INDEX

A

Agency, 59, 61
American Indians, remnants of Joseph, 41
Anderson, Joseph: on president Joseph Fielding Smith, 134; on revelation, 41
Andrew, the apostle, of the Jewish Twelve, 2, 5, 10
Apostasy: in the early days of the Church, 13, 57–59, 61, 66, 95; of Judas Iscariot, 11; of the Lamanites, 22
Apostles: Jewish Twelve, 1–13; Nephite Twelve, 16–22; sanctity of, 27
Apostolic succession, 11, 61
Area Authorities, instigation of, 157
Ashton, Marvin J., 155
Assistants to the Twelve, 152, 156, 162

B

Bailey, Langley A., 109
Ballard, Melvin J., 135–36, 154
Ballard, M. Russell, 135
Baptism, 4, 16–17, 19, 28, 31, 178
Bartholomew, the apostle, 2
Battle of Crooked River, 55
Bednar, David A., 169
Bennion, Adam S., 172
Benson, Ezra T., 61, 140
Benson, Ezra Taft: nomination of, 76; on apostleship, 172; on the apostate apostles, 58; on the sweetest association, 169; ordination of, 88, 140
Bible: Joseph Smith translation of, 5, 8, 10; King James Version of, 8
Book of Mormon, the, 17, 22, 31, 37–38, 59–60, 69, 103, 159, 177
Bowen, Albert E., 172
Boynton, John F., 38–40, 43, 58, 103

Index

Brown, Hugh B., 145–48, 155, 164, 172, 174–75

C

Callis, Charles A., 172
Cannon, Abraham H., 96, 117–18
Cannon, George Q., 55, 70–71, 82–87, 89, 96, 105–6, 115–18, 123, 151, 160, 171
Carrington, Albert, 95, 115
Carthage Jail, 60, 66, 162
Church Almanac, 92–93
Clark, J. Reuben, Jr., 151, 153–54
Clawson, Rudger, 120–25
Cowdery, Oliver, 9, 13, 31–34, 37, 40, 42, 58, 63, 93–94, 151
Cowley, Matthew, 118, 140–41, 172
Cowley, Matthias F., 118–20, 122, 125, 129, 141
Cullimore, James A., 178

D

Dedicatory prayer, 48–49
Dyer, Alvin R., ordination of, 98

E

Edersheim, Alfred, 3
Elias, 5, 8–9, 30, 93
Elijah, 8–10, 93
Endowment, 45–46, 48, 50–51, 66, 83
Essentials in Church History, 92, 119

Evans, Richard L., 163, 172
Excommunication, 59
Extermination order, 55

F

Faust, James E.: as an assistant to the Twelve, 155; on the sweet association of apostles, 169
First Presidency: of the early Church, 11–13, 80–82; of the restored church, 38, 41
First Vision, the, 23–30, 34–35

G

General conference, 37–38, 96, 98, 115, 121, 139, 145–47, 151, 173
Grant, Heber J., 58, 73–74, 88, 96–97, 111, 114–16, 118, 122, 125, 127, 130–32, 134–35, 138, 140, 145, 151–54 173–74
Grant, Heber Jeddy, 111–14
Grant, Jedediah M., 91–92, 112

H

Haight, David B., 155
Hales, Robert D., 155
Hannah, 133
Hardy, Rufus K., 141
Harris, Martin, 37, 39, 59
High Council, 26, 54, 67, 153
Hinckley, Alonzo A., 136–38
Hinckley, Gordon B.: on the priesthood, 73; on regional representatives, 156–57;

ordination of, 88, 148–49; special assistant, 155
Hunter, Howard W., 89, 149
Hyde, Orson, 38–41, 43, 46, 56–59, 65, 68, 79, 81
Hyde, William, 68

I

Infallibility, leaders never claim, 167–68
Isaiah, Nephite apostle, 17
Iscariot, Judas, 2, 11
Ivins, Anthony W., 115, 130–32

J

Jackman, Levi, 82
James, the apostle, 2–3, 7–9, 11–13, 18, 30–34, 82
James, brother of Jesus, the, 3, 12–13
Johnson, Luke S., 38–40, 43, 57
Johnson, Lyman E., 38–40, 43, 55, 58, 103
John, the Baptist, 5, 9, 31, 34
John, the Beloved, 1–4, 7–13, 18, 21, 30–34, 48–49, 82
Jonas, 17
Judas, 2

K

Kingdom of heaven, keys of the, 4, 6–7, 10
Kimball, Heber C.: grandfather of Spencer W. Kimball, 138; herald of grace, 79; mission to Britain, 56; ordination of, 38–40, 43, 60; visions of, 46, 48
Kimball, Spencer W.: called as president of the Church, 76; on changes in the Twelve and first presidency, 72; on Moses, 27–28; on the sweetest association, 169; ordination of, 73–75, 88, 138, 140
Kirtland Temple, 9, 45–49, 51–52, 93
Kumen, 17
Kumenonhi, 17

L

Lambson, Julina, 133
Law of Moses, 16–17, 19
Law, William, 59, 92
Lee, Harold B., 74–75, 88, 139–40, 145, 153–54, 159, 162–63, 176–78
Lehi, 19, 47, 159
Lund, Anthon H., 96, 116–18, 122, 125
Lyman, Amasa M., 61, 69, 95–96, 108,
Lyman, Francis M., 96, 113, 122, 130–31, 145–46, 162, 175

M

Magdalene, Mary, 2–3
Mark, the apostle, 2
Marks, William, 67

Marsh, Thomas B., 38–40, 43, 53–56, 101
Mathew, the apostle, 2, 10
Mathoni, the apostle, 17
Mathonihah, the apostle, 17
Matthias, the apostle, 11, 13, 43
Maxwell, Neil A., 155
McConkie, Bruce R., 1–3, 7–10, 13, 19–20, 24, 26, 33–34, 51, 133
McKay, David O., 74, 88, 97–98, 130, 140–41, 143, 145–49, 152, 154, 166–67, 175
McLellin, William E., 38–40, 43, 46–47, 56–57
Merrill, Joseph F., 172
Merrill, Marriner W., 96, 116–18, 122
Monson, Thomas S., 76
Morley, Isaac, 81
Morris, George Q., 155, 172
Moses, 7–10, 16–17, 19, 27, 30, 93, 167–68

N

Nelson, Russell M., 139
Nephi, 15–17
New York Prophet, 79

O

Ordinance: of baptism, 17; of the washing of feet, 45, 49–52

P

Packer, Boyd K., 60, 155, 164, 168, 173
Page, John E., 59, 80, 101
Paul, the apostle, 11–13, 164, 177
Patten, David W., 38–40, 43, 55, 58, 61
Penrose, Charles W., 127, 167
Perry, L. Tom, 155, 169
Peter, Simon: Cephas, 12; the apostle, 2–5, 6–11, 13, 17–18, 22, 30–34, 48, 82, 93, 130
Petersen, Mark E., 138, 170–71, 179
Phelps, William W., 42, 69, 79
Philip, the apostle, 2
Polygamy, suspension of, 128
Pratt, Orson, 38–40, 43, 57–58, 61, 80, 94
Pratt, Parley P., 38–40, 43, 57–58, 67, 69, 79, 105
Purifying, of the Twelve, 159, 161

Q

Quorum of the Seventy, 37, 64, 98, 155–56
Quorum of the Twelve, 6, 26–27, 35, 40, 47, 53, 55–56, 60–61, 64, 71–72, 76, 82, 85, 161–62, 169, 171–72, 175–76

R

Regional Representatives, 156–57
Revelation, rock of, 6
Rich, Charles, 115
Richards, Franklin D., 104
Richards, George F., 172
Richards, Stephen L., 172
Richards, Willard, 60–61, 79, 81–82, 94, 96, 101, 162
Rigdon, Sidney, 38, 40, 42, 48,

57, 59, 63–64, 66–70, 79, 81, 91–92
Roberts, B. H., 53, 134
Romney, George, 75–76, 116
Romney, Marion G., 144–45, 52–53, 55, 160, 162

S

Satellite broadcast, 173
School of the Prophets, 49–50
Shemnon, the apostle, 17
Simon, the apostle, 2
Smith, George A., 54, 60–61, 67, 79, 94, 97, 102–03
Smith, George Albert, 73, 88, 102, 124–25, 127
Smith, Hyrum, 60, 70, 82, 84, 92–93, 96, 125, 151
Smith, Hyrum Mack, 132
Smith, John Henry, 96, 102, 122, 124–26, 133
Smith, Joseph, Jr., 6–9, 13, 17, 22–23, 25, 28–35, 38, 40–42, 45–51, 57, 60–61, 63, 70, 73, 81–82, 93, 96, 101, 109, 114, 151
Smith, Joseph F., 18, 30, 39, 53, 80, 85–88, 91–93, 95–96, 107–10, 114, 117–19, 122–23, 125, 127, 130, 132–34, 160
Smith, Joseph Fielding, 11–12, 17–19, 22, 25, 28, 30, 32–33, 38, 43, 49, 56–57, 64, 69–70, 79–80, 86–88, 93, 95, 107, 115, 128, 132–35, 137–38, 178
Smith, William, 38–40, 43, 57, 61, 79

Snow, Eliza R., 111
Snow, Lorenzo, 29–30, 87–89, 96, 104, 109–10, 122, 127–29
Sperry, Sidney B., 15–17
Stapley, Delbert Leon, 143–44

T

Talmage, James E.: on apostleship, 27; on Peter, 4–5; on the Jewish Twelve, 2–4; on the priesthood, 9; on the primitive Church, 13; on the Savior, 11, 16, 22
Tanner, N. Eldon, 75–76, 139, 155, 167, 170
Taylor, John: ordination of, 60, 83–84, 85–87; sang to Joseph Smith, 60; champion of right, 79
Taylor, John W., 119–20, 122, 125, 129
Teasdale, George, 96, 114–16, 122, 125, 131
Thatcher, Moses, 96, 115
Thomas, the apostle, 2
Three Nephites, the 22
Three Witnesses, the, 27, 37–40, 43, 53, 55, 58–59, 81
Timothy, the apostle, 17
Tithing, 160
Translated beings, 9
Transfiguration, 8, 69
Trials, of mortality, 160
Twelve, serving as the First Presidency, 87–89

Index

U

Uchtdorf, Dieter F., 169

W

Wells, Daniel H., 91–92, 94–96, 151
Whitmer, David, 37, 39, 59, 151
Whitmer, Peter, 151
Whitney, Newel K., 40
Whitney, Orson F., 29, 127–29
Widtsoe, John A., 146, 172
Wight, Lyman, 35, 61, 80
Williams, Frederick G., 38, 40, 42, 59, 63–64, 81
Wirthlin, Joseph B., 156
Wonder, John R., 91
Woodruff, Abraham O., 101, 122, 125
Woodruff, Wilford, 25–26, 60, 65, 79–82, 84–88, 94–95, 101–02, 109–10, 116–18, 120, 129
Word of Wisdom, the, 160

Y

Young, Brigham: death of, 85; leads Saints to Utah, 61; Lion of the Lord, 79–80; one of the Twelve, 37–38, 40–41; on Joseph Smith, 33, 66; ordained his sons, 94; ordination of, 95; second apostle, 55; second prophet, 55; transfiguration of, 66, 69, 79
Young, Brigham, Jr., 94, 96–97, 122
Young, John W., 94
Young, Joseph, 37
Young, Zina D., 111

Z

Zedekiah, Nephite apostle, 17
Zion's Camp, 162

About the Author

Bruce E. Dana, an avid student of the gospel, served in the Northwestern States and Pacific Northwest Missions. He attended Weber State College and Utah State University. He has served in a variety of Church callings, and enjoys teaching the doctrines of the gospel.

He is the author of *Mysteries of the Kingdom; Mary, Mother of Jesus; Simon Peter; The Three Nephites and Other Translated Beings; Glad Tidings Near Cumorah;* and *The Eternal Father and His Son.*

Brother Dana is married to Brenda Lamb. Their family includes six daughters, two sons, and seventeen grandchildren. You can reach the author at bdana@pcu.net.